speak TIBETAN
like a Tibetan

speak TIBETAN
like a Tibetan

Dialogues in Colloquial Tibetan

Dhondup Tsering

SPEAK TIBETAN Like a Tibetan
Dhondup Tsering

Published by:
PILGRIMS PUBLISHING

An imprint of:
PILGRIMS BOOK HOUSE
(Distributors in India)
B 27/98 A-8, Nawabganj Road
Durga Kund, Varanasi-221010, India
Tel: 91-542-2314059, 2314060, 2312456
Fax: 91-542-2312788, 2311612
E-mail: pilgrims@satyam.net.in
Website: www.pilgrimsbooks.com

PILGRIMS BOOK HOUSE (New Delhi)
9 Netaji Subhash Marg, 2nd Floor
Near Neeru Hotel,
Daryaganj,
New Delhi 110002
Tel: 91-11-23285081
E-mail: pilgrim@del2.vsnl.net.in

Distributed in Nepal by:
PILGRIMS BOOK HOUSE
P O Box 3872, Thamel,
Kathmandu, Nepal
Tel: 977-1-4700942
Off: 977-1-4700919
Fax: 977-1-4700943
E-mail: pilgrims@wlink.com.np

New and Enlarged Edition 2004

Edited by Christopher N Burchett
Layout by Asha Mishra

ISBN: 81-7769-214-3

Printed in India at Pilgrim Press Pvt. Ltd. Lalpur, Varanasi

To my dear parents
for
all their sacrifices

Contents

Preface

Learning a new language is difficult but it can be exciting and rewarding later. Often boring at the beginning, it becomes more interesting as you cross the first stage. One feels like an early explorer not knowing what to expect around the next mountain or the next village. You keep discovering new things day after day. It is more like a journey with all the excitements involved in making a real one but without any dangers. As the intricacies of a language are slowly understood and the learner able to communicate, the mysteries surrounding a people and its culture are unravelled giving a valuable insight to whoever is passionate about them. It is an absolute must for anyone studying the history, culture, politics, arts, religion etc., of any country to learn the spoken language of that people.

Learning a language is also important for someone who intends to visit any foreign country. It makes his experience complete. By knowing the language of a place, even if not perfect, brings the visitor closer to the locals. It makes him/her less vulnerable to overcharging and unfortunate incidents. In a larger sense, it makes the world a closer and a friendlier place to live in.

For a long time, I felt the need to write a book for learning colloquial Tibetan; one that was sensitive to the needs of learners who are complete strangers to the language. A book that is at once easy to understand and also interesting at the same time. I have tried that in this book and in a way it has somewhat succeeded judging from the favourable response to the first edition of this book. It even received an offer to be translated into German.

This revised edition has some significant additions, the most important of which is the underlining of letters that have to be pronounced in a high tone with low aspiration. Such differences can have a major effect on whether a word is pronounced correctly or not. I have also added footnotes at the end of some pages to help learners with some tricky Tibetan words. I hope this book helps bridge the communication gap between Tibetans and the outside world.

I am indebted to Susan Marfield, USA for making this book possible. I would like to thank Ngawang Yeshe, Chemi Tenzin, Norbu Wangchuk, Phurbu Tsering and all my friends for their support and encouragement.

Dhondup Tsering
Dharamsala
July 2003

1
Pronunciation guide-I

ཀ	ka	king (c)
ཁ	kha	quiz (q)
ག	ga	god (g)
ང	nga	wrong (ng)
ཙ	cha	chat (ch)
ཚ	chha	NEE[1]
ཇ	ja	jump (j)
ཉ	nya	NEE
ཏ	ta	NEE
ཐ	tha	threat (th)
ད	dha	dharma (dh)
ན	na	name (n)
པ	pa	pop (p)

---

[1] No English Equivalent

ཕ	ph[2]	phrase (ph)
བ	ba	bread (b)
མ	ma	meet (m)
ཙ	tsa	parts (ts)
ཚ	tssa	tsunami (ts)
ཛ	za	zoo (z)
ཝ	wa	wait (w)
ཞ	shha	vision (s)
ཟ	sza	NEE
འ	'a	NEE
ཡ	ya	yes (y)
ར	ra	rain (r)
ལ	la	late (l)
ཤ	sha	sharp (sh)
ས	sa	sand (s)
ཧ	ha	hat (h)
ཨ	a	army (a)

---

[2] Pronounce 'p' with strong aspiration. Aspiration here means the amount of breadth blown in pronouncing a letter. Hold your palm close to your mouth and you will know.

There are five vowels in the Tibetan language like that of English. Unlike the English language, the Tibetan vowels are not represented by any letters but by entirely different symbols except in the case of the vowel 'a' which is represented by the final Tibetan alphabet. The other four vowels are:

◌	i	king (i)
◌	u	pull (u)
◌	e	bed (e)
◌	o	pot (o)

For the above Tibetan NEE words, we will explain them by giving examples of words that are nearest in equivalent.

ཚ   chha

The difference between cha and chha is same as that of between the sound of 'dh' in dharma and 'th' in threat. 'Dh' in dharma is pronounced in a higher tone when compared to 'th' in threat. While you pronounce 'cha' in a high tone as that of 'ch' in chat, you have to pronounce 'chha' in a lower tone and with a strong aspiration. The difference between the two can also be observed in the difference between 'k' as in 'kill' and 'q' as in quiz. 'cha' has to be pronounced like 'k' and 'chha' has to be pronounced like 'q'.

ཉ   nya

Catch the sound of 'ny' in canyon and you might come close to the original sound.

ཏ   ta

When learning to pronounce this letter, you have to take into consideration the difference between 'd' in drama and 'dh' in dharma. You

3

have to pronounce 'ta' like that of 'dh' in dharma but with a low
aspiration and not as that of 't' in truck or tent.

ཙ   tsa

The sound of 'rts' in parts comes close to the original. It has to be
pronounced in high tone.

ཚ   tssa

If you know how to pronounce tsunami, there is no problem. This
letter has to be pronounced with a strong aspiration. The difference
between the above two words is same as that of between 'dh' in
dharma and 'th' in threat.

ཞ   shha

Catch the sound of 's' in leisure and vision. If you pronounce 'sh' as
in sharp but with a strong aspiration like that of 'th' in threat, you will
come close to the sound of shha.

ཟ   sza

You can understand this letter easily once you know the difference
between 'sh' and 'shha'. Here the difference is between 's' as in
sand and 'sza'. Sza has to be pronounced like that of 's' but with a
strong aspiration like that of shha above.

འ   'a

Catch the sound of 'h' in 'wah' and you might just get lucky. When
this Tibetan letter is the base letter in a word, it will be indicated by

4

the English word 'w' and when this letter follows another base letter, it will be indicated by 'a'.

Note: Although the above examples might help readers depending upon the individual, the best solution for these NEE letters will be to find a Tibetan to help you learn them.

2
Pronunciation guide-II

Of the total 29 Tibetan alphabets, 14 are closely related in pronunciation; the only difference being whether they are pronounced with a strong aspiration or not. Take the case of the first two alphabets of the Tibetan language 'ka' and 'kha'. While 'k' in 'ka' is the same as 'k' in king (high tone, low aspiration), the latter 'kha' finds its equivalent in 'q' of quiz (low tone, high aspiration). While people not familiar with the Tibetan language may find them totally unrelated, Tibetans look at the two letters as similar in sound and indeed one find them together (except in the case of 'sha' 'shha' 'sa', and 'sza') in the order of the Tibetan alphabet.

high tone, low aspiration	low tone, high aspiration	low tone, moderate aspiration
ka	kha	ga
cha	chha	ja
ta	tha	dha
pa	pha	ba
tsa	tssha	za
sha	shha	
sa	sza	

Some of the Tibetan alphabets not in this group acquire similar characteristics as above when superscribed or subjoined or preceded by another letter most notably in the case of nga, nya, na, ma, and ya. Take for example the case of 'nga' meaning 'I' and '<u>nga</u>' meaning 'five'. Nga is in low tone with moderate aspiration while <u>nga</u> is in a high tone with low aspiration. All underlined letters should be pronounced in a high tone with low aspiration.

In the following I have made further list of Tibetan letters which when superscribed or subjoined by another letter makes an *entirely different sound* or a *similar sound* but with high or low aspiration in contrast to the sound of the base letter.

The following examples are three letters 'ka', 'kha' and 'ga' subjoined by the letter 'y'. It creates a new sound not found in the alphabets.

ཀྱ　　　ཁྱ　　　གྱ

'kya' can be pronounced like that of 'c' in cute.
'khya' can be pronounced like that of 'kya' but with strong aspiration.
'gya' can be pronounced like that of letter 'g' in regulate and not as in gun.
The following examples of 'ka', 'kha', 'ga', and 'ha' subjoined by the letter 'r'.

ཀྲ　　　ཁྲ　　　གྲ　　　ཧྲ

'tra' is pronounced like that of 't' in top. It will be indicated by the 'tr' letter combination in the following chapters.
'thra' is pronounced softly like of 't' in triumph. This will be indicated by the 'thr' letter combination.
'dra' is pronounced like that of 'd' in drama.
'rha' is pronounced like that of 'r' as in rock but with strong aspiration.

The letters 'ka' and 'sza' subjoined by the letter 'l'.

ཀླ　　　ཟླ

7

'l̲a' is pronounced like that of 'l' as in late but in a much higher tone and with low aspiration.

'dha' is pronounced like that of 'dh' in dharma.

3
Pronunciation guide-III

In Tibetan words, letters following vowels which comes after a base letter as in 'yodh' (stay) or 'drag' (rock) should not be stressed clearly like 'ck' in the name Jack. These letters are there to indicate how the vowels should be emphasized. The letters 'dh' indicate that you have to pronounce the preceding vowel as if it has 'dh' after it.

Let us take the example of the English word 'bang' (gunfire). Although there is the letter 'g' at the end, we don't pronounce it clearly as we would do in 'drug' or 'dig'. Even then the letter 'g' being there in the first place, we pronounce the word 'bang' in such a way that it automatically comes to our understanding that there is the letter 'g' at the end. Now imagine the same word without the letter 'g' at the end. Then it would be 'ban' which would sound completely different. Similar is the case with the above Tibetan words.

Although a first time language learner will have some difficulty in understanding such subtle features of the Tibetan language, it is best that they pronounce these letters softly.

Mey (ey)-Here emphasize the letter 'e' as in bed or red but without pronouncing 'd'. The stress of 'e' in red should be there in Mey.
Rey (ey)-Same as above.
Pey (ey)-As in Day or May in English.
Yodh[3] (o)-Here the stress on 'o' is important to indicate the presence of 'dh' after it. The 'dh' of course remains silent. Don't pronounce the word as in both.
Tra (ra)-The letter 'r' does not have to be pronounced as is truck or tray. 'Tr' should be pronounced as in take or tame.

---

3. The 'o' in 'yodh' should be pronounced like the German 'ø'.

4
Essential words[4]

Airport
nam-thang   གནམ་ཐང་།

Angry
khong-thro   ཁོང་ཁྲོ།

Age
lo   ལོ།

Address
kha-jang   ཁ་བྱང་།

Bus
lang[5]-khor/bas   རླངས་འཁོར། སྦ་སི།

Bridge
szam-pa   ཟམ་པ།

Boil
kol-wa   སྐོལ་བ།

---

4. The phonetics of some Tibetan words may not exactly correspond to the written Tibetan. This is deliberate because of differences between written and colloquial Tibetan.
5. All the underlined letters such as 'l' here indicate low aspiration and high tone.

Back
gyab-la ཀྱུབ།

Book
dheb དེབ།

Boy
bu བུ།

Carry
khyer-wa འཁྱེར་བ།

Careful
szab-szab གཟབ་གཟབ།

Camera
par-ches དཔར་ཆས།

Cloth
dhug-log དུག་སློག

Cold
drang-mo གྲང་མོ།

Cost
gong-tsse གོང་ཚད།

Country
lung-pa ལུང་པ།

Come
shog ཤོག

Door
go
སྒོ།

Far
thag-ring-po
ཐག་རིང་པོ།

Female
mo
མོ།

Friend
drog-po
གྲོགས་པོ།

Front
dhun
མདུན།

Fruit
shing-tog
ཤིང་ཏོག

Food
kha-lag
ཁ་ལག

Forget
je-pa
བརྗེད་པ།

Girl
bu-mo
བུ་མོ།

Go
gyug
རྒྱུགས།

God
lha
ལྷ།

Good
yag-po ཡག་པོ།

Goodbye
ga-le pheb-go ག་ལེ་ཕེབས་གོ

Happy
kyi-po སྐྱིད་པོ།

Help
rog-pa རོགས་པ།

Here
dhey-la དེ་ལ།

Him
kho ཁོ།

House
khang-pa ཁང་པ།

Hospital
men-khang སྨན་ཁང་།

Hot
tssa-wo ཚ་པོ།

Hotel
dron-khang མགྲོན་ཁང་།

Hungry
tog-pa ལྟོགས་པ།

Husband
khyo-ga   ཁྱོ་ག

I
nga   ང་།

In
nang-la   ནང་ལ།

Library
pe-zodh   དཔེ་མཛོད།

Listen
nyen-pa   ཉན་པ།

Love
ga   དགའ།

Male
pho   ཕོ།

Many
mang-po   མང་པོ།

Map
sa-thra   ས་ཁྲ།

Meaning
dhon   དོན་དག

Medicine
men   སྨན།

Monastery
gon-pa

དགོན་པ།

Money
ngul

དངུལ།

Name
ming

མིང་།

Near
dram-la/thri-la

འགྲམ་ལ། མཐྲིས་ལ།

New
sar-pa

གསར་པ།

Number
ang-ki

ཨང་ཀི།

Old
nying-pa

རྙིང་པ།

Out
chhi-la

ཕྱི་ལ།

Paper
shu-gu

ཤོག་བུ།

Passport
lag-khyer

ལག་འཁྱེར།

Pen
nyug-gu

སྙུག་གུ།

Plane
n̲am-dru

གནམ་གྲུ།

Please[6]
ku-chi

སྐུ་མཁྱེན།

Perhaps
chig-je-na

གཅིག་བྱས་ན།

Rain
chhar-pa

ཆར་བ།

Read
l̲og-pa

སློག་པ།

Restaurant
sza-khang

ཟ་ཁང་།

Road
lam

ལམ།

Sit
dhe-pa

བསྡད་པ།

See
thong-wa

མཐོང་བ།

Shop
tssong-khang

ཚོང་ཁང་།

---

6. Used when making a request.

Stand

lang-wa ལང་བ།

Student

lob-thruk སློབ་ཕྲུག

Sorry

gon-dhag དགོངས་དག

Table

chog-tse ཅོག་ཙེ།

Talk

ke-cha སྐད་ཆ།

Telephone

kha-par ཁ་པར།

Time

dhus[7]-tssodh དུས་ཚོད།

Tired

thang-chhe ཐང་ཆད།

Thanks

thuk-je-chhe ཐུགས་རྗེ་ཆེ།

They

khong-tsso ཁོང་ཚོ།

---

7. The 's' in 'dhus' is silent.

This
dhi འདི།

Toilet
sang-chodh གསང་སྤྱོད།

Top
tse རྩེ།

Train
ri-li or me-khor རི་ལི། མེ་འཁོར།

Travel agency
drim-drul les-khang འགྲིམ་འགྲུལ་ལས་ཁང་།

Umbrella
nyi-dhug ཉི་གདུགས།

Under
wog-la འོག་ལ།

Understand
go-tssodh-pa གོ་ཚོད་པ།

Use
be-chodh བེད་སྤྱོད།

Vacation
gung-seng གུང་སེང་།

Wait
gug-pa སྒུག་པ།

Want

go[8]   དགོས།

Water

chu   ཆུ།

We

nga-tsso   ང་ཚོ།

Wife

sza-dha   བཟའ་ཟླ།

Write

dris-pa   བྲིས་པ།

Weather

<u>n</u>am-shis   གནམ་གཤིས།

Yes

rey   རེད།

Note: In the Indian sub-continent where the majority of the Tibetan refugees live, a bus is called 'bas' (a loan word from English) and bus stations are called bas ti-sing. Ti-sing is a corruption of the English word 'station'. In central Tibet however, a bus is called <u>l</u>ang-khor and bus depots are called <u>l</u>ang-khor bab-tssug. Ri-li also is a corruption of the English word 'rail' and is used by Tibetans in exile.

---

8. The 'o' in 'go' like 'ø' in German.

5

First contact

When approaching a stranger for help or information use the following openers:

> Rin-po-che to a lama
> Ku-shok-la to a monk
> Ani-la to a nun
> Gen-la to someone older than you
> Jo-la to someone young (male)
> Acha-la to someone young (female)
> Bu-la to a boy
> Bumo-la to a girl

When approaching someone familiar to you, use 'la' which is an honorific term much like sir after his or her name. For e.g.,

> Tashi-la
> Pema-la

You can also use Ta-shi de-lek which means good luck. This is a good opener to greet both strangers and friends. There are other openers indicating time like:

Good morning

<u>n</u>ga-dro dhe-lek   སྔ་དྲོ་བདེ་ལེགས།

Good afternoon

nyin-gung dhe-lek   ཉིན་གུང་བདེ་ལེགས།

Good evening
gon-dro dhe-lek

དགོང་དྲོ་བདེ་ལེགས།

Male
pho

ཕོ།

Choephel
chhos-phel

ཆོས་འཕེལ།

Damdul
dram-dhul

དག་འདུལ།

Dawa
dha-wa

ཟླ་བ།

Dhargyal
dhar-gyal

དར་རྒྱལ།

Dhondup
dhon-drup

དོན་གྲུབ།

Gyalpo
gyal-po

རྒྱལ་པོ།

Gyaltsen
gyal-tssen

རྒྱལ་མཚན།

Gyatso
gya-tsso

རྒྱ་མཚོ།

Jamyang

jam-yang འཇམ་དབྱངས།

Karma

kar-ma སྐར་མ།

Kalsang

kel-sang སྐལ་བཟང་།

Lobsang

lob-sang བློ་བཟང་།

Namgyal

ṉam-gyel རྣམ་རྒྱལ།

Ngawang

nga-wang ངག་དབང་།

Norbu

nor-bu ནོར་བུ།

Palden

pal-dhen དཔལ་ལྡན།

Passang

pa-sang པ་སངས།

Phuntsok

phun-tssok ཕུན་ཚོགས།

Penpa

pen-pa སྤེན་པ།

22

Sangpo

szang-po   བཟང་པོ།

Sonam

so-nam   བསོད་ནམས།

Tashi

ta-shi   བཀྲ་ཤིས།

Tenpa

ten-pa   བསྟན་པ།

Tenzin

ten-zin   བསྟན་འཛིན།

Tsering

tsse-ring   ཚེ་རིང་།

Thupten

thup-ten   ཐུབ་བསྟན།

Ugen

u-gen   ཨུ་རྒྱན།

Wangyal

wan-gyal   དབང་རྒྱལ།

Wangchuk

wang-chuk   དབང་ཕྱུག

Yeshi

ye-shi   ཡེ་ཤེས།

Female
mo   མོ།

Bhuti
bu-ti   བུ་ཁྲིད།

Chime
chhi-me   འཆི་མེད།

Choekyi
chho-kyi   ཆོས་སྐྱིད།

Choezom
chho-zom   ཆོས་འཛོམས།

Choedon
chho-don   ཆོས་སྒྲོན།

Dikyi
dhi-kyi   བདེ་སྐྱིད།

Dolker
dol-kar   སྒྲོལ་དཀར།

Dolma
dol-ma   སྒྲོལ་མ།

Kunsang
kun-sang   ཀུན་བཟང་།

24

Kyizom

kyi-zom ཀྱིད་འཛོམས།

Lhamo

lha-mo ལྷ་མོ།

Norzom

no-zom ནོར་འཛོམས།

Palzom

pel-zom དཔལ་འཛོམས།

Paldon

pel-don དཔལ་སྒྲོན།

Pema

pe-ma པདྨ།

Wangmo

wang-mo དབང་མོ།

Yangzom

yang-zom དབྱངས་འཛོམས།

Yangchen

yang-chen དབྱངས་ཅན།

Yangkyi

yang-kyi དབྱངས་སྐྱིད།

Youdon

yu-don གཡུ་སྒྲོན།

25

Dialogue-I

Good morning

nga-dro dhe-lek

སྐུ་རྡོ་བདེ་ལེགས།

Do you speak English?

khye-rang in-ke shes-gi yo-pey.[9]

ཁྱེད་རང་དབྱིན་སྐད་ཤེས་ཀྱི་ཡོད་པས།

Yes but very little.

yag-po shes-gi mey.

ཡག་པོ་ཤེས་ཀྱི་མེད།

What is your name?

khye-rang ming ga-re yin.

ཁྱེད་རང་གི་མིང་ག་རེ་ཡིན།

My name is Dhondup.

ngey ming Dhon-dup yin.

ངའི་མིང་ལ་དོན་གྲུབ་ཡིན།

How are you?

khye-rang ku-szug dhe-po yin-pey.

ཁྱེད་རང་སྐུ་གཟུགས་བདེ་པོ་ཡིན་པས།

I am fine.

nga dhe-po yin.

ང་བདེ་པོ་ཡིན།

Please come inside.

yar pheb-nang.

ཡར་ཕེབས་གནང་།

Thank you.

thuk-je-chhe.

ཐུགས་རྗེ་ཆེ།

---

9. Ke should be pronounced like 'ca' in cage and shes as 'sha' in shade. The 's' that follows the vowel 'e' is silent in shes.

Where are you from?
khye-rang lung-pa ga-nes[10] yin.

ཁྱེད་རང་ལུང་པ་ག་ནས་ཡིན།

I am from USA.
nga A-ri nes-yin

ང་ཨ་རི་ནས་ཡིན།

Are you here on vacation?
khye-rang dhey gung-seng la pheb-pa yin-pey.

ཁྱེད་རང་འདིར་གུང་སེང་ལ་ཕེབས་པ་ཡིན་པས།

Yes.
la-wong.

ལ་འོང་།

How long do you plan to stay in India?
khye-rang gya-gar-la yun ring-los[11] shhug-ye yin.

ཁྱེད་རང་རྒྱ་གར་ལ་ཡུན་རིང་ལོས་ལྷུགས་ཡེ་ཡིན།

Only one month.
dha-wa chig-rang-chig.

ཟླ་བ་གཅིག་རང་གཅིག

Only one month?
dha-wa chig lab-pey.

ཟླ་བ་གཅིག་ལས།

Yes. I want to go to Africa also.
wong. nga Africa ley dro-go yodh.

འོང་། ཨཕ་རི་ཀ་ལའང་འགྲོ་དགོས་ཡོད།

I have to go now.
dha-nga dro-go yodh.

ད་ང་འགྲོ་དགོས་ཡོད།

Goodbye.
ga-le pheb-go.

ག་ལེ་ཕེབས་གོ

---

10. The 'ne' in 'nes' should be pronounced like 'le' in less with 'ss' silent. Words like 'les' 'ches' etc should be pronounced in a similar way.
11. The 's' in 'los' is silent and the 'o' as 'ø' in German.

27

Dialogue-II

Nice weather
nam-shis yag-po dhug.

གནམ་གཤིས་ཡག་པོ་འདུག

So hot today.
dhey-ring tssa-wa shhe-dra dhug.

དེ་རིང་ཚ་བ་ཞེ་དྲག་འདུག

Nice place.
sa-cha yag-po dhug.

ས་ཆ་ཡག་པོ་འདུག

Yes. It is a nice place.
dhug. sa-cha yag-po dhug.

འདུག ས་ཆ་ཡག་པོ་འདུག

Where are you from?
khye-rang lung-pa ga-nes yin-pey.

ཁྱེད་རང་ལུང་པ་ག་ནས་ཡིན

I am from France.
nga France-nes yin.

ཕརནས་ས་ནས་ཡིན

Does it rain a lot there?
france-la chhar-pa mang-po gyab-gi re-pey.

ཕརནས་སི་ལ་ཆར་པ་མང་པོ་རྒྱག་གི་རེད་པས

No. Why?
ma-rey. ga-re yin-na.

མ་རེད། ག་རེ་ཡིན་ན

Here it rains a lot.
dhey-la chhar-pa mang-po gyab-gi rey.

དེ་ལ་ཆར་པ་མང་པོ་རྒྱག་གི་རེད

You must buy an umbrella.
khye-rang nyi-dhug chig nyo-go rey.

ཁྱེད་རང་ཉི་གདུགས་གཅིག་ཉོ་དགོས་རེད

28

I will.
nyo-gi yin-dha.

ཉོ་གི་ཡིན་དྭ།

Are you visiting India for the first time?
gya-gar-la pheb-pa theng[12] dhang-po yin-pey.

རྒྱ་གར་ལ་ཕེབས་པ་ཐེངས་དང་པོ་ཡིན་པས།

Sorry. Say that again.
gon-dhag. go-nes lab-dhang.

དགོངས་དག གོ་ནས་ལབ་དང་།

Can you speak more slowly?
khye-rang ke-cha lhodh-lhodh[13] she-rog nang.

ཁྱེད་རང་སྐད་ཆ་ལྷོད་ལྷོད་ཤོད་རོགས་གནང་།

This is my first visit to India.
nga gya-gar yong-wa theng dhang-po yin.

ང་རྒྱ་གར་ཡོང་བ་ཐེངས་དང་པོ་ཡིན།

What do you do?
khye-rang ga-re je-gi yodh.

ཁྱེད་རང་ག་རེ་བྱེད་ཀྱི་ཡོད།

What?
ga-re.

ག་རེ།

Do you work?
chhag-les nang-gi yo-pey.

ཕྱག་ལས་གནང་གི་ཡོད་པས།

Yes.
wong.

འོང་།

Where?
ga-wa-la.

ག་བར་ལ།

---

12. The 'th' in 'theng' should be pronounced like 'th' in theatre.
13. The 'dh' in lhodh is silent. The 'o' as in German 'ø'. The 'lh' should be pronounced like the usual 'l' but with strong aspiration and low tone.

As a teacher in TCV school.
TCV-la ge-gen yin.

ཊེ་སི་སེ་ལ་དགེ་རྒན་ཡིན།

And you?
khye-rang.

ཁྱེད་རང་།

I am a writer.
nga dheb tsom-pa-po yin.

ང་དེབ་རྩོམ་པ་པོ་ཡིན།

Where are you staying?
ga-wa shhug-gi yodh.

ག་བ་ཞུགས་ཀྱི་ཡོད།

I am staying at Hotel Tibet.
bodh-gi sza-khang-la dhe-gi yodh.

བོད་ཀྱི་མགྲོན་ཁང་ལ་སྡོད་ཀྱི་ཡོད།

How is Dharamsala?
dha-ram-sa-la ga-dre[14] dhug.

ད་རམ་ས་ལ་ག་འདྲ་འདུག

It is a very nice place.
sa-cha yag-po dhug.

ས་ཆ་ཡག་པོ་འདུག

There are so many tourists here.
tro-chham-pa mang-po shhe-dra dhug.[15]

སྒྲོ་འཆམས་པ་མང་པོ་ཞེ་དྲག་འདུག

You meet many people here.
dhey-la mi mang-po thug-gi rey.

དེ་ལ་མི་མང་པོ་ཐུག་གི་རེད།

How long have you been here?
dhey-la leb-nes nyi-ma ga-tssodh chhin-song.

དེ་ལ་སླེབས་ནས་ཉི་མ་ག་ཚོད་ཕྱིན་སོང་།

_____

14. Dre, Dra and dro in the sentences that follows should be pronounced as 'd' in drama with no emphasis on 'r'. Dre as in day, dra as 'da' in dart, and dro as 'do' in doe.

15. Pronounce the 'u' in 'dhug' as 'oo' in look with the 'g' silent.

About a week.
dhun-thrag[16] chig-tsam chhin-song.

བདུན་ཕྲག་གཅིག་ཙམ་ཕྱིན་སོང་།

I have to meet someone.
nga mi-chig thug-go yodh.

ང་མི་གཅིག་ཐུག་དགོས་ཡོད།

It was nice meeting you.
khye-rang thug-nes ga-wo shhe-dra jung.

ཁྱེད་རང་ཐུག་ནས་དགའ་པོ་ཞེ་དྲག་བྱུང་།

When shall we meet again?
nga-nyi yang-kyar ga-dhus thug-ge.

ང་གཉིས་ཡང་བསྐྱར་ག་དུས་ཐུག་གས།

Same place tomorrow.
sang-nyin. sa-cha dhi-ga rang-la.

སང་ཉིན། ས་ཆ་འདི་ག་རང་ལ།

See you.
jel-yong.

མཇལ་ཡོང་།

Dialogue-III

Hello
ha-lo

ཧ་ལོ།

Let us go and have tea.
ja thung-ga dro.

ཇ་འཐུང་ག་འགྲོ།

Let us go to Om hotel.
om sza-khang-la dro.

ཨོམ་ཟ་ཁང་ལ་འགྲོ།

---

16. The 'th' in 'thrag' should be pronounced like 't' in treat with the 'g' silent.

Can I smoke here?
dhey-la tha-ma thung chhog-gi re-pey.

དེ་ལ་ཐ་མག་འཐུང་ཆོག་གི་རེད་པས།

Of course.
yin-dha-yin.

ཡིན་ད་ཡིན།

I want to smoke too.
nga-ye tha-ma thung-gi yin.

ང་ཡེ་ཐ་མག་འཐུང་གི་ཡིན།

Can you please smoke outside?
khye-rang tha-ma chhi-la thung-rog nang.

ཁྱེད་རང་ཐ་མག་ཕྱི་ལ་འཐུང་རོགས་གནང་།

Sorry.
gon-dhag.

དགོངས་དག

Are you married?
chhang-sa gyab tssar yin-pey.

ཆང་ས་བརྒྱབ་ཚར་ཡིན་པས།

No, I am single.
gyab-mey. nga rhang-rhang[17] yin.

རྒྱག་མེད། ང་རྱང་རྱང་ཡིན།

How old are you?
khye-rang lo ga-tssodh yin.

ཁྱེད་རང་ལོ་ག་ཚོད་ཡིན་པས།

I am 37.
nga lo so-dhun yin.

ང་ལོ་སོ་བདུན་ཡིན།

You look very young.
khye-rang shhon-shhon thong-gi dhug.

ཁྱེད་རང་གཞོན་གཞོན་མཐོང་གི་འདུག

---

17. The 'rh' in 'rhang' like normal 'r' with strong aspiration.

Do I?
dhug-ge.

འདུག་གས།

Are you free tomorrow?
sang-nyin les-ka yo-pey.

སང་ཉིན་ལས་ཀ་ཡོད་པས།

We will go to Bhagsu Nath tomorrow.
sang-nyin bag-su-nath-la dro.

སང་ཉིན་བག་སུ་ནག་ལ་འགྲོ།

It is a nice place by the riverside.
dhi chhu thri[18]-la sa-cha kyi-po chig yo-rey.

དེ་ཆུ་མཐིས་ལ་ས་ཆ་སྐྱིད་པོ་ཞིག་ཡོད་རེད།

There is also a beautiful waterfall.
dhey-la bab-chhu nying-je-po chig yo-rey.

དེ་ལ་འབབ་ཆུ་སྙིང་རྗེ་པོ་ཞིག་ཀྱང་ཡོད་རེད།

How far is it?
thag-ring-los yo-rey.

ཐག་རིང་ལོས་ཡོད་རེད།

It is about 20 minutes walk.
kar-ma nyi-shu gom-pa gyab-na leb-gi rey.

སྐར་མ་ཉི་ཤུ་གོམ་པ་རྒྱབ་ན་སླེབས་ཀྱི་རེད།

We will go there tomorrow.
sang-nyin dhey-la dro.

སང་ཉིན་དེ་ལ་འགྲོ།

I should go now.
dha-nga dro-go yodh.

ད་ང་འགྲོ་དགོས་ཡོད།

It is getting dark.
nag-gung chhag-gi dhug.

ནག་ཁྱུང་ཆགས་ཀྱི་འདུག

---

18. The 'thr' in 'thri' should be pronounced like 'tr' in treat.

It is too early now.
dhan-ta nga-po rey.

ད་ལྟ་སྔ་པོ་རེད།

I am coming too.
nga-ye yong-gi yin.

ང་ཡེ་ཡོང་གི་ཡིན།

I will pay.
ngul nge tre[19]-go.

དངུལ་ངས་སྤྲོད་གོ

Good night.
szim-ja nang-go.

གཟིམ་འཇག་གནང་གོ

Dialogue-IV

What is the matter?
ga-re je-song.

ག་རེ་བྱུས་སོང་།

Nothing.
ge je-ma-song.

གེ་བྱེད་མ་སོང་།

What do you want?
khye-rang la ga-re go-pey?

ཁྱེད་རང་ལ་ག་རེ་དགོས་པས།

I want to talk to you.
khye-rang nyam-dhu ke-cha she-dhodh yodh.[20]

ཁྱེད་རང་མཉམ་དུ་སྐད་ཆ་ཤོད་འདོད་ཡོད།

Why are you angry?
khye-rang khong-thro ga-re je-nes sza-song.

ཁྱེད་རང་ཁོང་ཁྲོ་ག་རེ་བྱས་ནས་ཟ་སོང་།

---

19. The 'tr' in 'tre' should be pronounced as 't' in Tibet.
20. The 'dh' in yodh and dhodh is silent. The 'o' as in German 'ø'.

You are late.
khye-rang chhi-po leb-song.
ཁྱེད་རང་ཕྱི་པོ་སླེབས་སོང་།

I am in a hurry.
nga drel-wa yodh.
ང་བྲེལ་བ་ཡོད།

I am feeling cold.
nga khyag-gi dhug.
ང་འཁྱག་གི་འདུག

I am tired.
nga ka-les khag-song.
ང་དཀའ་ལས་ཁག་སོང་།

I am disappointed.
nga lo pham-song.
ང་བློ་ཕམ་སོང་།

I can't do this.
dhi-nga je thub-sa ma-rey.
འདི་ང་བྱེད་ཐུབ་ས་མ་རེད།

Do you understand me?
ha-go song-wey.
ཧ་གོ་སོང་བས།

Perfectly.
go yag-po tssodh-song.
གོ་ཡག་པོ་ཚོད་སོང་།

Do you know this person?
khye-rang mi-dhi ngo shes-gi yo-pey.
ཁྱེད་རང་མི་འདི་ངོ་ཤེས་ཀྱི་ཡོད་པས།

Not very well.
ngo yag-po shes-gi mey.
ངོ་ཡག་པོ་ཤེས་ཀྱི་མེད།

Please write this down.
ku-chi. dhi dri-rog nang.
སྐུ་མཁྱེན། འདི་འབྲི་རོགས་གནང་།

What is the meaning of this?
dhi ga-re rey.

འདི་ག་རེ་རེད།

You should leave now.
dha khye-rang pheb-rog nang.

ད་ཁྱེད་རང་ཕེབས་རོགས་གནང་།

6
Eating and Drinking

Dialogue-I

Are you hungry?
tog-gi dhug-ge.

 སྟོགས་ཀྱི་འདུག་གས།

Yes. Let us eat somewhere.
wong. kha-lag sza-ga dro.

འོང་། ཁ་ལག་བཟའ་ས་འགྲོ།

Where shall we go?
ga-wa dro-ge.

ག་པར་འགྲོ་གས།

Let us go to Tibet restaurant.
bodh-gi sza-khang-la dro.

བོད་ཀྱི་ཟ་ཁང་ལ་འགྲོ།

How is the food there?
kha-lhag ga-dre yo-rey.

ཁ་ལག་ག་འདྲས་ཡོད་རེད།

It is excellent.
yag-po shhe-dra yo-rey.

ཡག་པོ་ཞེ་དྲག་ཡོད་རེད།

What do you want?
ga-re chhodh-gi yin-pey.

ག་རེ་མཆོད་ཀྱི་ཡིན་པས།

I love rice.
nga dre-la ga-po yodh.

ང་འབྲས་ལ་དགའ་པོ་ཡོད།

37

I don't like meat.
nga sha-la ga-po mey.

ང་ཤ་ལ་དགའ་པོ་མེད།

I am thirsty.
nga kha kom-gi dhug.

ང་ཁ་སྐོམ་གྱི་འདུག

Have a coke.
coke thung-nang.

ཀོག་འཐུང་གནང་།

I will have a beer.
nga-la bi-yar chig tre-rog nang.

ང་ལ་བི་ཡར་གཅིག་སྤྲོད་རོགས་གནང་།

We don't serve beer here.
nga-tsso bi-yar tsong-gi mey.

ང་ཚོ་བི་ཡར་ཚོང་གི་མེད།

I will have a milk tea.
nga-la ja-chig tre-rog nang.

ང་ལ་ཇ་གཅིག་སྤྲོད་རོགས་གནང་།

Do you serve Tibetan food?
bodh-pey kha-lhag szo-gi yo-pey.

བོད་པའི་ཁ་ལག་བཟོ་གི་ཡོད་པས།

Can we have the menu.
kha-lag ming-shhung ton-rog nang.

ཁ་ལག་མིང་གཞུང་སྟོན་རོགས་གནང་།

We serve Tibetan food.
bodh-pey kha-lhag yodh.

བོད་པའི་ཁ་ལག་ཡོད།

Have thukpa.
thuk-pa chhodh-dhang.

ཐུག་པ་མཆོད་དང་།

I am a vegetarian.
nga sha sza-gi mey.

ང་ཤ་བཟའ་བའི་མེད།

38

We have special vegetable thukpa.
nga tssor tssel-thukpa mig-sel yodh.

ང་ཚོར་ཚལ་ཐུག་པ་དམིགས་གསལ་ཡོད།

Can I have a glass of water?
chhu phor-ba gang tre-rog nang.

ཆུ་ཕོར་པ་གང་སྤྲོད་རོགས་གནང་།

Do you have Tibetan butter tea?
bodh-ja yo-pey.

བོད་ཇ་ཡོད་པས།

Yes, but it will take some time.
yodh. yi-nay dhus-tssodh tog-tsam gor-gi rey.

ཡོད། ཡིན་ནའི་དུས་ཚོད་ཏོག་ཙམ་འགོར་གྱི་རེད།

The bill, please.
ngul-zin tre-rog nang.

དངུལ་འཛིན་སྤྲོད་རོགས་གནང་།

Keep the change.
ngul lhag-ma khye-rang nyar-nang.

དངུལ་ལྷག་མ་ཁྱེད་རང་ཉར་གནང་།

Dialogue-II

Hello! You must be very happy.
ha-lo. khye-rang kyi-po shhe-dra yo-gi rey.

ཧ་ལོ། ཁྱེད་རང་སྐྱིད་པོ་ཞེ་དྲག་ཡོད་ཀྱི་རེད།

Why?
ga-re je-nes.

ག་རེ་བྱས་ནས།

You have been promoted.
khye-rang go-nes phar-shhag.

ཁྱེད་རང་གོ་གནས་འཕར་ཤག

Let us celebrate tonight.
dhey-ring gon-dhag nga-tsso kyi-po tang-go.

དེ་རིང་དགོང་དག་ང་ཚོ་སྐྱིད་པོ་གཏང་གོ

39

Where?
ga-wa-la.
ག་པར་ལ།

In Hotel Tibet.
bodh-gi sza-khang nang-la.
བོད་ཀྱི་ཟ་ཁང་ནང་ལ།

We will meet at 6 pm today.
gon-dhag chhu-tssodh druk-pa-la thug-go.
དགོང་དག་ཆུ་ཚོད་དྲུག་པ་ལ་ཐུག་གོ

Is everyone here?
mi tssang-ma leb dhug-ge.
མི་ཚང་མ་སླེབས་འདུག་གས།

Yes.
dhug.
འདུག

Give me one large whiskey peg.
nga-la whiskey peg chhe-wa chig tre-rog nang.
ཝིས་ཀི་པེག་ཆེ་བ་གཅིག་སྤྲོད་རོགས་གནང་།

I will have a beer.
nga bi-yar thung-gi yin.
ང་བི་ཡར་འཐུང་གི་ཡིན།

I want to drink chang.
nga chhang thung-gi yin.
ང་ཆང་འཐུང་གི་ཡིན།

Go to Majnukatilla.
Man-ju-ti-lar gyug.
མན་ཇུ་ཏི་ལར་རྒྱུགས།

Where is the liquor shop?
a-rak tssong-khang ga-wa yo-rey.
ཨ་རག་ཚོང་ཁང་ག་པར་ཡོད་རེད།

Near the bus stand.
bas ti-sing thri-la yo-rey.
རླངས་འཁོར་འབབ་ཚུགས་འགྲམ་ལ་ཡོད་རེད།

Give me a bottle of whiskey.
whiskey shel-dham chig tre-rog nang.

ཤེལ་གི་ཤེལ་དམ་གཅིག་སྤྲོད་རོགས་གནང་།

Which one?
ga-dhi.

ག་འདི།

Scotch whiskey.
scotch whiskey.

སོ་ཀོཆ་ཨ་རག

How much?
gong ga-tssodh rey.

གོང་ག་ཚོད་རེད།

Rs.550.
gor nga-gya nga-chu.

སྒོར་ལྔ་བརྒྱ་ལྔ་བཅུ།

Thanks.
thuk-je chhe.

ཐུགས་རྗེ་ཆེ།

VOCABULARY

Alcohol
a-rak

ཨ་རག

Bread
bag-leb

བག་ལེབ།

Butter
mar

མར།

Boiled
khol-ma

འཁོལ་མ།

41

Beer
bi-yar
པི་ཡར།

Breakfast
shhog-ja
ཞོགས་ཇ།

Chair
kup-kyag
ཀུབ་བཀྱག

Chopstick
kho-tse
ཁོ་ཙེ།

Cold
drang-mo
གྲང་མོ།

Curd
shho
ཞོ།

Cup
phor-pa
ཕོར་པ།

Dry
kam-po
སྐམ་པོ།

Egg
go-nga
སྒོ་ང་།

Fresh
sos-pa
སོས་པ།

Fried
ngos-kyog
བརྔོས་ཀྱོག

Food
kha-lag
ཁ་ལག

42

Garlic

gog-pa

སྒོག་པ།

Glass

shel-phor

ཤེལ་ཕོར།

Hot

tssa-wo

ཚ་པོ།

Milk

wo-ma

འོ་མ།

Meat

sha

ཤ།

Plate

dher-ma

དེར་མ།

Oily

shhag-zi

ཞག་ཅེ།

Potato

shho-gog

ཞོ་བོག།

Restaurant

sza-khang

ཟ་ཁང་།

Rice

dre

འབྲས།

Salt

tssa

ཚ།

Salad

drang-tssel

གྲང་ཚལ།

43

Sour

kyur-mo སྐྱུར་མོ།

Soup

kho-wa ཁུ་བ།

Spicy

me-na སྨན་སྣ།

Sweet

ngar-mo མངར་མོ།

Steam-cook

lang-tsos རླངས་བཙོས།

Spoon

thur-ma ཐུར་མ།

Table

chog-tse ཅོག་ཙེ།

Tea

ja ཇ།

Vegetable

tssel ཚལ།

Water

chhu ཆུ།

Note: Dinner is called gon-dhag kha-lhag and lunch nyin-gung kha-lag. Kha-lag means food and gon-dhag and nyin-gung means evening and daytime. Bar is called a-rak thung-sa. It means a place where one can consume alcohol.

7
Work and Play

Dialogue-I

Where do you work?
khye-rang chhag-les ga-wa nang-gi yodh.

ཁྱེད་རང་ཕྱག་ལས་ག་པར་གནང་གི་ཡོད།

I work in a factory.
nga szo-drey nang les-ka je-gi yodh.

ང་བཟོ་གྲྭའི་ནང་ལས་ཀ་བྱེད་ཀྱི་ཡོད།

When do you go to work?
chhag-les nang-ga ga-dhus pheb-gi yodh.

ཕྱག་ལས་གནང་ག་ག་དུས་ཕེབས་ཀྱི་ཡོད།

I go to work at 8 a.m. in the morning.
shhog-ge chhu-tssodh gye-pa-la.

ཞོགས་པ་ཆུ་ཚོད་བརྒྱད་པ་ལ།

When do you reach your workplace?
chhag-les nang-sar ga-dhus leb-gi dhug.

ཕྱག་ལས་གནང་སར་ག་དུས་སླེབས་ཀྱི་འདུག

9 a.m.
chhu-tssodh gu-pa-la leb-gi dhug.

ཆུ་ཚོད་དགུ་པར་སླེབས་ཀྱི་འདུག

It is 15 minutes by bus.
bas nang-la dro-na kar-ma cho-nga gor-gi rey.

རྣངས་འཁོར་ནང་ལ་འགྲོ་ན་སྐར་མ་བཅོ་ལྔ་འགོར་གྱི་འདུག

45

I work from 9 a.m. to 5 p.m.
nga shhog-ge chhu-tssodh gu-pa nes nga-pa bar les-ka je-gi yodh.

ང་ཞོགས་པ་ཆུ་ཚོད་དགུ་པ་ནས་ལྔ་པ་བར་ལས་ཀ་བྱེད་ཀྱི་ཡོད།

Isn't there a lunch break?
nyin-gung kha-lag gi bar-seng yo ma-re-pey.

ཉིན་གུང་ཁ་ལག་གི་བར་གསེང་ཡོད་མ་རེད་པས།

It is from 1 p.m. to 2 p.m.
nyin-gung chhu-tssodh dhang-po nes nyi-pa bar rey.

ཉིན་གུང་ཆུ་ཚོད་དང་པོ་ནས་གཉིས་པ་བར་རེད།

How much is your salary?
khye-rang la la-cha ga-tssodh ra-gi dhug.

ཁྱེད་རང་ལ་གླ་ཆ་ག་ཚོད་རག་གི་འདུག

It is Rs.4000 per month.
dha-wa-la gor shhi-tong ra-gi dhug.

ཟླ་བ་ལ་སྒོར་བཞི་སྟོང་རག་གི་འདུག

Dialogue-II

We work in the same office.
nga-nyi les-khung chig-pa rey.

ང་གཉིས་ལས་ཁུང་ཅིག་པ་རེད།

She works in a school.
mo lob-drey nang les-ka je-gi yo-rey.

སློབ་གྲྭའི་ནང་ལས་ཀ་བྱེད་ཀྱི་ཡོད་རེད།

She is very busy.
mo-rang les-key drel-wa shhe-dra yo-rey.

མོ་རང་ལས་ཀའི་བྱེལ་བ་ཞེ་དྲག་ཡོད་རེད།

He works hard.
kho-rang les-ka hur-po yo-rey.

ཁོ་རང་ལས་ཀ་ཧུར་པོ་ཡོད་རེད།

I am unemployed.
nga les-mey yin

ང་ལས་མེད་ཡིན།

My sister is a teacher.

ngey a-chag ge-gen rey.

ངའི་ཨ་ལྕགས་དགེ་རྒན་རེད།

He is lazy.

kho-rang les-ka gyi-po yo-ma-rey.

ཁོ་རང་ལས་ཀ་སྐྱིད་པོ་ཡོད་མ་རེད།

I don't work on weekends.

nga sza pen-pa dhang nyi-mar les-ka je-gi mey.

ང་གཟའ་སྤེན་པ་དང་ཉི་མར་ལས་ཀ་བྱེད་ཀྱི་མེད།

Dialogue-III

Do you like your job?

les-ka ga-dre dhug.

ལས་ཀ་ག་འདྲས་འདུག

Yes. I do.

yag-po dhug.

ཡག་པོ་འདུག

Is it interesting?

les-ka kyi-po dhug-ge.

ལས་ཀ་སྐྱིད་པོ་འདུག་གས།

No, but it pays a lot.

min-dhug. yi-nay la-cha yag-po dhug.

མིན་འདུག ཡིན་འང་ལྒ་ཆ་ཡག་པོ་འདུག

How is your boss?

khye-rang gi u-zin ga-dre dhug.

ཁྱེད་རང་གི་དྦུ་འཛིན་ག་འདྲས་འདུག

He is a very kind man.

kho-rang mi szang-po rey.

ཁོ་རང་མི་བཟང་པོ་རེད།

How are your colleagues?

khye-rang gi les-rog ga-dre dhug.

ཁྱེད་རང་གི་ལས་རོགས་ག་འདྲས་འདུག

47

I don't talk to them.
nga kho-tsso nyam ke-cha shes-gi mey.

ང་ཁོ་ཚོ་མཉམ་སྐད་ཆ་ཤོད་ཀྱི་མེད།

Why?
ga-re je-nes.

ག་རེ་བྱས་ནས།

They are all animals.
kho-tsso tssang-ma sem-chen rey.

ཁོང་ཚོ་ཚང་མ་སེམས་ཅན་རེད།

Animals?
sem-chen.

སེམས་ཅན།

I work in a zoo.
nga chen-szig-khang nang les-ka je-gi yodh.

ང་སྐྱུན་གཟིགས་ཁང་ནང་ལས་ཀ་བྱེད་ཀྱི་ཡོད།

Dialogue-IV

How do you spend your Sundays?
khye-rang sza nyi-mar ga-re nang-gi yodh.

ཁྱེད་རང་གཟའ་ཉི་མར་ག་རེ་གནང་གི་ཡོད།

I go for swimming.
nga chhu gel-ga dro-gi yodh.

ང་ཆུ་བརྒྱལ་ག་འགྲོ་གི་ཡོད།

What about you?
khye-rang.

ཁྱེད་རང་།

I play football.
nga kang-tse po-lo tse-gi yodh.

ང་ཀང་རྩེད་པོ་ལོ་རྩེ་གི་ཡོད།

Where do you play football?
kang-pol ga-wa tse-gi yodh.

ཀང་པོལ་ག་པར་རྩེ་གི་ཡོད།

48

At the school's playground.
lob-drey thang-la.

སློབ་གྲྭའི་ཐང་ལ།

I love basketball.
nga lag-tse po-lo ga-wo yodh.

ང་ལག་རྩེད་པོ་ལོ་ལ་དགའ་བོ་ཡོད།

I also love basketball.
nga-ye lag-pol ga-wo yodh.

ང་ཡང་ལག་པོལ་ལ་དགའ་བོ་ཡོད།

We will organise a basketball match this Sunday.
nga-tssο sza nyi-mar lag-pol dren-dhur chig go-drig je-go.

ང་ཚོ་གཟའ་ཉི་མ་འདིར་ལག་པོལ་འགྲན་བསྡུར་ཞིག་གོ་སྒྲིག་བྱེད་དགོ

We don't have any uniforms.
nga-tsso-la drig-chhe mey.

ང་ཚོ་ལ་སྒྲིག་ཆས་མེད།

You can wear white t-shirts.
khye-rang tsso gan-ji kar-po gon.

ཁྱེད་རང་ཚོ་གན་ཇི་དཀར་པོ་གོན།

Do we need to wear halfpants?
ha-pen gon-go re-pey.

ཧ་པན་གོན་དགོས་རེད་པས།

You can if you want.
gon-na drig-gi rey.

གོན་ན་འགྲིག་གི་རེད།

Dialogue-V

Where do you plan to spend your annual holiday this year?
khye-rang tsso dha-lo gung-seng ga-wa tang-tsis[21] yodh.

ཁྱེད་རང་ཚོ་ད་ལོ་གུང་སེང་ག་པར་གཏང་རྩིས་ཡོད།

---

21. The 's' in 'tsis' is silent.

We are going to Tibet.
nga-tsso bodh-la dro-tsis yodh.

ང་ཚོ་བོད་ལ་འགྲོ་རྩིས་ཡོད།

When?
ga-dhus.

ག་དུས།

At the end of May.
chi-dha nga-pey dha-jug-la.

ཕྱི་ཟླ་ལྔ་པའི་ཟླ་མཇུག་ལ།

It is good to visit Tibet during summer.
bodh-la yar-ka dro-na yag-po yo-rey.

བོད་ལ་དབྱར་ཀ་འགྲོ་ན་ཡག་པོ་ཡོད་རེད།

We are also going to spend a week in Nepal.
nga-tsso bel-yul-la dhun-thrag chig dhe-tsis yodh.

ང་ཚོ་བལ་ཡུལ་ལ་བདུན་ཕྲག་གཅིག་བསྡད་རྩིས་ཡོད།

Are you planning to climb Mt. Everest?
khye-rang tsso Jo-mo lang-ma gang zag-tsis yo-pey.

ཁྱེད་རང་ཚོ་ཇོ་མོ་གླང་མའི་སྒང་འཛེགས་འཆར་ཡོད་པས།

Yes and that too naked.
dhug-log mey-nes zag-tsis yodh.

དུག་སློག་མེད་ནས་འཛེགས་རྩིས་ཡོད།

We also plan to do some cycling in Nepal.
bel-yul-la kang-khor tang-nes chham-chham dro-tsis yodh.

བལ་ཡུལ་ལ་ཀང་འཁོར་གཏང་ནས་འཆམ་འཆམ་འགྲོ་རྩིས་ཡོད།

Nepal is very hot during summer.
yar-ka bel-yul-la tssa-wa shhe-dra yo-rey.

དབྱར་ཀ་བལ་ཡུལ་ལ་ཚ་བ་ཞེ་དྲག་ཡོད་རེད།

We are not going to visit China.
nga-tsso gya-nag-la dro-tsis mey.

ང་ཚོ་རྒྱ་ནག་ལ་འགྲོ་རྩིས་མེད།

We might go to India.
nga-tsso chig-je-na gya-gar-la dro-gi yin.

ང་ཚོ་གཅིག་བྱས་ན་རྒྱ་གར་ལ་འགྲོ་གི་ཡིན།

Perhaps we will hire a car.

chig-je-na nga-tsso mo-tra[22] le–tsis yodh.

གཅིག་བྱས་ན་ང་ཚོ་མོ་ཊ་གླས་ རྩིས་ཡོད།

VOCABULARY

Occupation

tsso-les   འཚོ་ལས།

Teacher

ge-gen   དགེ་རྒན།

Reporter

sar-godh-pa   གསར་འགོད་པ།

Photographer

par-pa   དཔར་པ།

Barber

tra-shhar   སྐྲ་བཞར།

Businessman

tssong-pa   ཚོང་པ།

Cook

ma-jen   མ་བྱན།

Secretary

drung-yig   དྲུང་ཡིག

---

22. Mo-tra is a corruption of the English word 'motor'. 'Tra' is pronounced like 't' in take.

Translator
ke-gyur

སྐད་བསྒྱུར།

Driver
kha-lo-wa

ཁ་ལོ་བ།

Peon
yig-kyel

ཡིག་སྐྱེལ།

Accountant
tsis-pa

རྩིས་པ།

Cashier
ngul-nyer

དངུལ་གཉེར།

Lawyer
trim-tsodh-pa

ཁྲིམས་རྩོད་པ།

Editor
tsom-drig-pa

རྩོམ་སྒྲིག་པ།

Nurse
men-pa

སྨན་པ།

Doctor
em-ji

ཨེམ་ཆི།

Postman
drag-kyel

སྦྲག་སྐྱེལ།

Mechanic
mo-tra szo-khen

མོ་ཊ་བཟོ་མཁན།

Workplace

les-ka je-sa

ལས་ཀ་བྱེད་ས།

Bank

ngul-khang

དངུལ་ཁང་།

Shop

tssong-khang

ཚོང་ཁང་།

Factory

szo-dra

བཟོ་གྲྭ།

Office

yig-tssang

ཡིག་ཚང་།

School

lob-dra

སློབ་གྲྭ།

Court

thrim-khang

ཁྲིམས་ཁང་།

Hotel

sza-khang

ཟ་ཁང་།

Library

pe-zodh

དཔེ་མཛོད།

Note: Writers are called dheb tsom-pa-po. Dheb means books and tsom-pa-po means writer. Similarly Librarians are called pe-zodh dho-dham-pa. pe-zodh means library and do-dham-pa means someone who is in charge of the library.

Weather
nam-shis   གནམ་གཤིས།

Dry
kam-po   སྐམ་པོ།

Cold
drang-mo   གྲང་མོ།

Hot
tssa-wo   ཚ་པོ།

Wet
lon-pa   རློན་པ།

Heavy rainfall
chhar-pa chhen-po   ཆར་པ་ཆེན་པོ།

Heavy snowfall
gang mang-po   གངས་མང་པོ།

Freezing
ha-chang drang-mo   ཧ་ཅང་གྲང་མོ།

Sunny
nyi-ma yag-po shar-wa   ཉི་མ་ཡག་པོ་ཤར་བ།

Humidity
shha-tssen   ཞ་ཚན།

Fog
mug pa   སྨུག་པ།

Windy
lung-tssub   རླུང་ཚུབ།

Overcast
nam-thrig-pa

གནམ་འཐིག་པ།

Clear sky
nam thang-pa

གནམ་དངས་པ།

Thunder
druk-ke

འབྲུག་སྐད།

Hail
ser-wa

སེར་བ།

Dark
nag-gung

ནག་ཁུང་།

Pitch-black
nag-gung nag-kyang

ནག་ཁུང་ནག་ཀྱང་།

Daylight
nyin-gung

ཉིན་གུང་།

Weather forecast
nam-shis ngon-dha

གནམ་གཤིས་སྔོན་བདོ།

Seasons
nam-dhus

ནམ་དུས།

Spring
chidh-ka

དཔྱིད་ཀ

Summer
yar-ka

དབྱར་ཁ།

Autumn
ton-ka
སྟོན་ཀ

Winter
gun-ka
དགུན་ཀ

Time
dhus-tssodh
དུས་ཚོད

Second
kar-chha
སྐར་ཆ

Minute
kar-ma
སྐར་མ

Hour
chhu-tssodh
ཆུ་ཚོད

Morning
shhog-pa
ཞོགས་པ

Afternoon
nyin-gung
ཉིན་གུང

Evening
gon-dro
དགོང་དྲོ

Day
nyin-mo
ཉིན་མོ

Night
gon-dhag
དགོང་མོ

56

Yesterday

dhang-gong · མདང་གོང་།

Today

dhey-ring · དེ་རིང་།

Tomorrow

sang-nyin · སང་ཉིན།

Day after tomorrow

nang-nyin · གནངས་ཉིན།

Last week

dhun-thrag ngon-ma · བདུན་ཕྲག་སྔོན་མ།

Next sunday

sza nyi-ma je-ma · གཟའ་ཉི་མ་རྗེས་མ།

This year

dha-lo · ད་ལོ།

As soon as possible

gang gyog-gyog · གང་མགྱོགས་མགྱོགས།

Immediately

lam-seng · ལམ་སེང་།

Right now

dhan-ta-rang · ད་ལྟ་རང་།

One o'clock

chhu-tssodh dhang-po · ཆུ་ཚོད་དང་པོ།

57

Twelve noon
nyin-gung chhu-tssodh chu-nyi
ཉིན་གུང་ཆུ་ཚོད་བཅུ་གཉིས།

Twelve midnight
gon-dhag chhu-tssodh chu-nyi
དགོང་དག་ཆུ་ཚོད་བཅུ་གཉིས།

Quarter past seven
dhun-dhang kar-ma cho-nga
བདུན་དང་སྐར་མ་བཅོ་ལྔ།

Half past eight
gye dhang chhe-ka
བརྒྱད་དང་ཕྱེད་ཀ

Quarter to nine
gu-pa szim-par kar-ma cho-nga
དགུ་པ་ཟིན་པར་སྐར་མ་བཅོ་ལྔ།

Five past three
sum dhang kar-ma nga
གསུམ་དང་སྐར་མ་ལྔ།

Twenty to four
shhi-pa szim-par kar-ma nyi-shu
བཞི་པ་ཟིན་པར་སྐར་མ་ཉི་ཤུ།

A minute to midnight
gon-dhag chhu-tsodh chu-nyi szim-pa kar-ma chig
དགོང་དག་ཆུ་ཚོད་བཅུ་གཉིས་ཟིན་པ་སྐར་མ་གཅིག

Seven o'clock in the morning
shhog-ge chhu-tssodh dhun-pa
ཞོགས་པ་ཆུ་ཚོད་བདུན་པ།

Two in the afternoon
nyin-gung chhu-tssodh nyi-pa
ཉིན་གུང་ཆུ་ཚོད་གཉིས་པ།

58

Half past six in the evening
gon-dhag chhu-tssodh druk dhang chhe-ka
དགོང་དག་ཆུ་ཚོད་དྲུག་དང་ཕྱེད་ཀ།

Days of the week
sza   གཟའ།

Monday
sza dha-wa   གཟའ་ཟླ་བ།

Tuesday
sza mig-mar   གཟའ་མིག་དམར།

Wednesday
sza lhak-pa   གཟའ་ལྷག་པ།

Thursday
sza phur-bu   གཟའ་ཕུར་བུ།

Friday
sza pa-sang   གཟའ་པ་སངས།

Saturday
sza pen-pa   གཟའ་སྤེན་པ།

Sunday
sza nyi-ma   གཟའ་ཉི་མ།

Twelve months of a year
dha-wa chu-<u>nyi</u>   ཟླ་བ་བཅུ་གཉིས།

January
chi-dha[23] dhang-po   ཕྱི་ཟླ་དང་པོ།

February
chi-dha <u>nyi</u>-pa   ཕྱི་ཟླ་གཉིས་པ།

March
chi-dha sum-pa   ཕྱི་ཟླ་གསུམ་པ།

April
chi-dha shhi-pa   ཕྱི་ཟླ་བཞི་པ།

May
chi-dha <u>nga</u>-pa   ཕྱི་ཟླ་ལྔ་པ།

June
chi-dha druk-pa   ཕྱི་ཟླ་དྲུག་པ།

July
chi-dha dhun-pa   ཕྱི་ཟླ་བདུན་པ།

August
chi-dha gye-pa   ཕྱི་ཟླ་བརྒྱད་པ།

September
chi-dha gu-pa   ཕྱི་ཟླ་དགུ་པ།

---

23. Chi-dha (literally outside month) means months according to the western calendar. The Tibetan calendar months are called bodh-dha.

60

October

chi-dha chu-pa

ཕྱི་ཟླ་བཅུ་པ།

November

chi-dha chu-chig

ཕྱི་ཟླ་བཅུ་གཅིག

December

chi-dha chu-<u>nyi</u>

ཕྱི་ཟླ་བཅུ་གཉིས།

8

The family

Dialogue-I

Do you have a photo of your family?
khye-rang nang-mi par yo-pey.

ཁྱེད་རང་གི་ནང་མིའི་དཔར་ཡོད་པས།

Yes. Here it is.
yodh. dhey-la szig-dhang.

ཡོད། དེ་ལ་གཟིགས་དང་།

Where are your parents?
khye-rang gi pha-ma nyi ga-wa.

ཁྱེད་རང་གི་ཕ་མ་གཉིས་ག་པར་འདུག

These are my parents.
dhi-nyi ngey pha-ma rey.

འདི་གཉིས་ངའི་ཕ་མ་རེད།

They look so young.
shhon-shhon rey dhug-ga.

གཞོན་གཞོན་རེད་འདུག་ག

This photo is quite old.
par dhi nying-pa rey.

དཔར་འདི་རྙིང་པ་རེད།

What does your father do?
pa-la chhag-les ga-re nang-gi yo-rey.

ཕ་ལགས་ཕྱག་ལས་ག་རེ་གནང་གི་ཡོད་རེད།

He is retired. He used to be a soldier.
khong ge-yol rey. ngon-ma mag-mi rey.

ཁོང་རྒས་ཡོལ་རེད། སྔོན་མ་དམག་མི་རེད།

62

Who is that old man?
po-la dhi su-rey.

པོ་ལགས་འདི་སུ་རེད།

That is my grandfather.
dhi ngey po-po-la rey.

འདི་ངའི་པོ་པོ་ལགས་རེད།

Who is he holding?
khong su-yi lag-pa szin-nes dhe dhug-ge.

ཁོང་སུའི་ལག་པ་ཟིན་ནས་བསྡད་འདུག་གས།

That is my kid sister.
ngey sing-mo chhung-wa rey.

ངའི་སྲིང་མོ་ཆུང་བ་རེད།

Don't you have any aunt?
khye-rang la su-mo me-pey.

ཁྱེད་རང་ལ་སུ་མོ་མེད་པས།

No, but I have one uncle.
mey. yi-nay a-gu chig yodh.

མེད། ཡིན་འང་ཨ་ཁུ་གཅིག་ཡོད།

He is not in this photo.
khong par-dhi nang-la yo-ma-rey.

ཁོང་དཔར་འདི་ནང་ལ་ཡོད་མ་རེད།

Dialogue-II

Are you married?
khye-rang chhang-sa gyab-tssar yin-pey.

ཁྱེད་རང་ཆང་ས་བརྒྱབ་ཚར་ཡིན་པས།

Yes. Sir.
la-wong.

ལ་འོང་།

Who is your husband?
khye-rang gi khyo-ga su-rey.

ཁྱེད་རང་གི་ཁྱོ་ག་སུ་རེད།

Passang is my husband.
ngey khyo-ga Passang rey.

ངའི་ཁྱོ་ག་པ་སངས་རེད།

Do you have any children.
khye-rang nyi-la thru-gu yo-pey.

ཁྱེད་རང་གཉིས་ལ་ཕྲུ་གུ་ཡོད་པས།

We have two sons.
nga-nyi-la bu-nyi yodh.

ང་གཉིས་ལ་བུ་གཉིས་ཡོད།

No daughters?
bu-mo me-pey.

བུ་མོ་མེད་པས།

No. Unfortunately.
mey. lo pham-pa chig-la.

མེད། ཕྲོ་ཕམ་པ་གཅིག་ལ།

How old are your children?
khye-rang nyi-gi thru-gu lo ga-tssodh rey?

ཁྱེད་རང་གཉིས་ཀྱི་ཕྲུ་གུ་ལོ་ག་ཚོད་རེད།

One is 8 and one is 11.
chig lo gye-dhang chig lo chu-chig rey.

གཅིག་ལོ་བརྒྱད་དང་གཅིག་ལོ་བཅུ་གཅིག་རེད།

Do you spend any time with your children?
thru-gu nyam-dhu dhus-tssodh kyel-gi yo-pey.

ཕྲུ་གུ་མཉམ་དུ་དུས་ཚོད་སྐྱེལ་གྱི་ཡོད་པས།

I don't get the time.
nga-la dhus-tssodh ra-gi min-dhug.

ང་ལ་དུས་ཚོད་རག་གི་མིན་འདུག

Dialogue-III

Where do you live?
khye-rang ga-wa shhug-gi yodh.

ཁྱེད་རང་ག་པར་བཞུགས་ཀྱི་ཡོད།

64

I live at home with my parents.
nga pha-ma nyam-dhu nang-la dhe-gi yodh.

ང་ཕ་མ་མཉམ་དུ་ནང་ལ་སྡོད་ཀྱི་ཡོད།

Where is your house?
khye-rang gi khang-pa ga-wa yo-rey.

ཁྱེད་རང་གི་ཁང་པ་ག་པར་ཡོད་རེད།

It is on the road to the library.
pe-zodh dro-sey lam-la yo-rey.

དཔེ་མཛོད་འགྲོ་སའི་ལམ་ལ་ཡོད་རེད།

Do you have a garden?
khye-rang nang-la dhum-ra yo-pey.

ཁྱེད་རང་ནང་ལ་ལྡུམ་ར་ཡོད་རེད་པས།

No. We have some flowers in pot.
mey. yi-nay za-ma nang me-tok kha-shes yodh.

མེད། ཡིན་འང་ཟ་མ་ནང་མེ་ཏོག་ཁ་ཤས་ཡོད།

How big is your house?
khang-pa chhe-los yodh.

ཁང་པ་ཆེ་ལོས་ཡོད།

There are six rooms.
khang-mig druk yo-rey.

ཁང་མིག་དྲུག་ཡོད་རེད།

How is the water supply?
chhu yag-po leb-gi dhug-ge.

ཆུ་ཡག་པོ་སླེབས་ཀྱི་འདུག་གས།

It is okay.
chhu yag-po leb-gi dhug.

ཆུ་ཡག་པོ་སླེབས་ཀྱི་འདུག

Dialogue-IV

Let us go to my house.
ngey nang-la dro.

ངའི་ནང་ལ་འགྲོ།

Isn't it locked?

go gyab yo ma-re-pey.

སྒོ་རྒྱག་ཡོད་མ་རེད་པས།

The key is with our neighbour.

dhe-mig khyim-tsse-la yo-rey.

དེ་མིག་ཁྱིམ་མཚེས་ལ་ཡོད་རེད།

Where are your parents?

khye-rang gi pha-ma nyi ga-wa yo-rey.

ཁྱེད་རང་གི་ཕ་མ་གཉིས་ག་པར་ཡོད་རེད།

They left for Delhi.

khong-tsso dhi-lir dro-song.

ཁོང་ཚོ་དི་ལིར་འགྲོ་སོང་།

I am all alone.

nga chig-po yin.

ང་གཅིག་པོ་ཡིན།

I want to eat something.

nga chig sza-dhodh dhug.

ང་གཅིག་བཟའ་འདོད་འདུག

Go in the kitchen.

thab-tssang nang-la gyug.

ཐབ་ཚང་ནང་ལ་རྒྱུགས།

Where is the bathroom?

thrus[24]-khang ga-wa yo-rey.

ཁྲུས་ཁང་ག་པར་ཡོད་རེད།

It is behind the kitchen.

thab-tssang gyab-la yo-rey.

ཐབ་ཚང་རྒྱབ་ལ་ཡོད་རེད།

Switch on the light.

dhang-po log-par.

དང་པོ་སློག་སྤར།

---

24. The 's' in 'thrus' is silent.

66

VOCABULARY-THE FAMILY

Young
shhon-shhon གཞོན་གཞོན།

Old
ge-khog རྒས་འཁོགས།

Male
pho ཕོ།

Female
mo མོ།

Husband
khyo-ga ཁྱོ་ག།

Wife
sza-dha བཟའ་ཟླ།

Boy
bu བུ།

Girl
bu-mo བུ་མོ།

Man
kye-pho སྐྱེས་ཕོ།

Woman
bu-mey བུད་མེད།

Children
thru-gu

ཕྲུ་གུ།

Grandfather
po-po

པོ་པོ།

Grandmother
mo-mo

མོ་མོ།

Father
pha

ཕ།

Mother
ma

མ།

Son
bu

བུ།

Daughter
bu-mo

བུ་མོ།

Uncle (p*)
agu

ཨ་ཁུ།

Uncle (m*)
a-shhang

ཨ་ཞང་།

Aunty (p)
a-ni

ཨ་ནི།

Aunty (m)
su-mo

སུ་མོ།

Brother (o*)

jo-lag རྗོ་ལགས།

Brother (y*)

chung-po གཅུང་པོ།

Sister (o)

a-chag ཨ་ཅག

Sister (y)

chung-mo གཅུང་མོ།

Nephew

tssa-wo ཚ་བོ།

Niece

tssa-mo ཚ་མོ།

* p=paternal, m=maternal, y=younger, o=older

VOCABULARY-HOME AND AROUND

Altar

chhodh-shom མཆོད་གཤོམ།

Ashtray

tha-ma dhab-sa ཐ་མག་འདབ་ས།

Bed

nyel-thri ཉལ་ཁྲི།

Blanket

nyel-chhe ཉལ་ཆས།

Box
gam སྒམ།

Broom
chhag-ma ཕྱགས་མ།

Bulb
shel-tog ཤེལ་ཏོག

Candle
yang-la ཡང་ལ།

Comb
gyug-she ཅྐྱུག་ཤད།

Curtain
thra-yol ཁྲ་ཡོལ།

Door
go སྒོ།

Envelope
yig-kog ཡིག་སྐོགས།

Electricity
log གློག

Fire
me མེ།

Flask
ja-dham ཇ་དམ།

Flashlight
log-shhu གློག་བཞུ།

Frying pan
tsse-lang ཚལ་སྣོད།

Home
nang ནང་།

House
khang-pa ཁང་པ།

Ink
nag-tssa སྣག་ཚ།

Kettle
khu-ti ཤོག་སྒྲིར།

Kitchen
thab-tssang ཐབ་ཚང་།

Knife
dri གྲི།

Ladle
kyog སྐྱོགས།

Lamp
sa-shhu གསལ་བཞུ།

Litter
ge-<u>ny</u>ig གད་སྙིགས།

Match
tsag-dra ཙ་སྒྲ།

Mirror
shel-go ཤེལ་སྒོ།

Nail
szer-ga   གཟེར་ག

Pillow
nge-go   སྔས་མགོ

Room
khang-mig   ཁང་མིག

Scissor
jam-tse   འཇབ་ཙེ

Soap
yi-tsi   ཡི་ཚི

Toothbrush
so-trus   སོ་ཁྲུས

Toothpaste
so-men   སོ་སྨན

Umbrella
nyi-dhug   ཉི་གདུགས

Utensil
nodh-ches/thab-ches   སྣོད་ཆས། ཐབ་ཆས།

Window
gi-gung   སྐེའུ་ཁུང་།

9

Doing the shopping

Dialogue-I

Where can I buy a toothpaste?
so-<u>me</u>n nyo-sa ga-wa yo-rey.

སོ་སྨན་ནོ་ས་ག་པར་ཡོད་རེད།

It is in that shop.
tssong-khang phi-ge-la yo-rey.

ཚོང་ཁང་ཕ་གི་ལ་ཡོད་རེད།

Do you sell toothpaste?
khye-rang la so-<u>me</u>n tsong-ye yo-pey.

ཁྱེད་རང་ལ་སོ་སྨན་ཚོང་རྒྱུ་ཡོད་པས།

Yes sir. We have different kind of toothpaste.
la-yodh. so-<u>me</u>n dra-mi-dra yodh.

ལ་ཡོད། སོ་སྨན་འདྲ་མི་འདྲ་ཡོད།

Can I have one Colgate toothpaste?
nga-la kol-gate so-<u>me</u>n tre-rog <u>n</u>ang.

ང་ལ་ཀོལ་གེ་ཊེ་སོ་སྨན་སྤྲད་རོགས་གནང་།

Big or small?
chhe-chhung gang-go.

ཆེ་ཆུང་གང་དགོས།

Medium.
dring-wa dhi-go.

འབྲིང་བ་འདི་དགོས།

How much?
gong ga-tssodh rey.

གོང་ག་ཚོད་རེད།

Rs.35
gor sum-chu so-<u>nga</u>.

སྒོར་སུམ་ཅུ་སོ་ལྔ། །

Why is it so expensive?
gong chhen-po dhi-dre ga-re rey.

གོང་ཆེན་པོ་འདི་འདྲ་ག་རེ་རེད། །

I said rupees not dollars.
gya-gar ngul lab-yin. dro-lar lab-mey.

རྒྱ་གར་སྒོར་མོ་ལབ་ཡིན། །སྒྲོ་ལར་ལབ་མེད། །

Dialogue-II

I want to buy a shirt.
nga todh-thung chig nyo-go yodh.

ང་སྟོད་ཐུང་གཅིག་ཉོ་དགོས་ཡོད། །

We will go to that big store.
tssong-khang chhen-po pha-gi nang-la dro.

ཚོང་ཁང་ཆེན་པོ་ཕ་གི་ནང་ལ་འགྲོ། །

Can you show me that red shirt?
todh-thung mar-po dhi ton-rog <u>n</u>ang.

སྟོད་ཐུང་དམར་པོ་འདི་སྟོན་རོགས་གནང་། །

It is too small.
bedh-dhe chhung-dra shhag.

འདི་བེད་དེ་ཆུང་དྲགས་ཤག །

Try this.
dhi ta-dhang.

འདི་ལྟ་དང་། །

It looks old.
dhi <u>n</u>ying-pa dra-po dhug.

འདི་རྙིང་པ་འདྲ་པོ་འདུག །

May I try this on.
dhi ta-na drig-gi re-pey.

འདི་ལྟ་ན་འགྲིག་གི་རེད་པས། །

How much is the price?
gong ga-tssodh rey.

གོང་ག་ཚོད་རེད།

Rs.500. It is the best quality.
gor nga-gya. gyu-cha yag-shos dhi-rey.

སྒོར་ལྔ་བརྒྱ། རྒྱུ་ཆ་ཡག་ཤོས་འདི་རེད།

Will you give discount if I buy two shirts?
todh-thung nyi nyos-na gong chag-gi re-pey.

སྟོད་ཐུང་གཉིས་ཉོས་ན་གོང་གཆག་གི་རེད་པས།

No.
chag-gi ma-rey.

མ་རེད།

Dialogue-III

There is a hole on this shirt.
todh-thung dhi re-shhag

སྟོད་ཐུང་འདི་རལ་ཞག

Where?
ga-wa-la.

ག་པར་ལ།

Here. At the back.
dhey. gyab-la.

དེ། རྒྱབ་ལ།

Let us go and return this.
dhi phar log-ga dro.

འདི་ཕར་བསློག་ག་འགྲོ།

Sir. There is a hole on this shirt.
gen-la. todh-thung dhi re-shhag.

རྒན་ལགས། སྟོད་ཐུང་འདི་རལ་ཞག

Take another shirt.
todh-thung shhen-pa len.

སྟོད་ཐུང་གཞན་པ་གཆིག་ལེན།

75

We want our money back.
ngul tssur tre-rog nang.

དངུལ་ཚུར་སློད་རོགས་གནང་།

We don't refund money once something is bought.
cha-lag nyo-tssar na ngul log-gi ma-rey.

ཅ་ལག་ཉོས་ཚར་ན་དངུལ་བསློག་གི་མ་རེད།

Okay. We will change this shirt for that green one.
a-les. dhey-dra yin-na todh-thung jang-gu pha-gi tre-rog
nang.

ཨ་ལས། དེ་འདྲ་ཡིན་ན་སྟོད་ཐུང་ལྗང་ཁུ་པ་གི་སློད་རོགས་གནང་།

Thank you.
thuk-je-chhe.

ཐུགས་རྗེ་ཆེ།

VOCABULARY

Bag

to-phe[25]   སློ་ཕད།

Big

chhen-po   ཆེན་པོ།

Bigger

chhe-wa   ཆེ་བ།

Biggest

chhe-shos   ཆེ་ཤོས།

Bunch

chhag-pa   ཆག་པ།

---

25. The 'e' in 'phe' like 'e' in red.

Buy
nyos-pa

ཉོས་པ།

Change
sil-ma

གསིལ་མ།

Discount
chhe-chag

ཕྱེད་ཆག ཆག་ཡང་།

Empty
tong-pa

སྟོང་པ།

Factory
szo-dra

བཟོ་གྲ།

Few
nyung-nyung

ཉུང་ཉུང་།

Full
gang

གང་།

Half
chhe-ka

ཕྱེད་ཀ

Handmade
lag-szos

ལག་བཟོས།

Heavy
jidh-po

ལྗིད་པོ།

Length
ring-tsse

རིང་ཚད།

Light
yang-po

ཡང་པོ།

77

Long
ring-po རིང་པོ།

Medium
dring-dring འབྲིང་འབྲིང་།

New
sar-pa གསར་པ།

Old
nying-pa རྙིང་པ།

Plenty
mang-po མང་པོ།

Polythene
gyig-shog འགྱིག་ཤོག

Price
gong གོང་།

Quality
pu-tsse སྤུས་ཚད།

Quarter
shhi-chha-chig བཞི་ཆ་གཅིག

Refund
chhir-log ཕྱིར་སློག

Sell
tsong-wa ཚོང་བ།

Short
thung-thung ཐུང་ཐུང་།

Small
chhung-chhung ཆུང་ཆུང་།

Smaller
chhung-wa ཆུང་བ།

Smallest
chhung-shos ཆུང་ཤོས།

Special
mig-sel དམིགས་གསལ།

Thick
thug-po མཐུག་པོ།

Thin
thra-wo ཕྲ་པོ།

Tight
dham-po དམ་པོ།

Weight
jidh-kog ལྗིད་གོག

Width
shheng-ga ཞེང་ཁ།

Colour
tsson-thra **ཚོན་ཁྲ།**

Black
nag-po ནག་པོ།

Blue.
ngon-po སྔོན་པོ།

Brown

gya-muk ཀྱུ་སྨུག

Grey

thal-dhog ཐལ་མདོག

Green

jang-khu ལྗང་ཁུ

Orange

li-wang ལི་ཝང་།

Pink

szing-kya ཟིང་སྐྱ

Purple

mu-men སྨུག་མེན།

Red

mar-po དམར་པོ།

Silver

ngul-dhog དངུལ་མདོག

White

kar-po དཀར་པོ།

Yellow

ser-po སེར་པོ།

Fabric

re-chha རས་ཆ།

Cotton

trin-bel སྤྲིན་བལ།

Leather
ko-wa གོ་བ།

Brocade
gos-chen གོས་ཆེན།

Wool
bel བལ།

Clothes
dhug-log དུག་སློག

Belt
kye-rag སྐེ་རག

Blouse
wog-joo འོག་འཇུག

Bra
nu-shub ནུ་ཤུབས།

Coat
kor གོར།

Earring
a-long ཨ་ལོང་།

Glove
lag-shub ལག་ཤུབས།

Handkerchief
lag-re ལག་རས།

Hat
shha-mo ཞྭ་མོ།

81

Raincoat
chhar-kheþ

ཆར་ཞིབས།

Ring
tsssi-kho

ཙིགས་ཞིབས།

Scarf
kha-tri

ཁ་དཀྲིས།

Shirt
todh-thung

སྟོད་གྱུང་།

Shoe
ham-go

ལྷམ།

Shoelace
ham-dro

ལྷམ་སྐྲོག

Socks
om-su

ཨོ་སྒུ། ཀང་སྒུ།

Trouser
gu-thung

གོས་གྱུང་།

Meat
sha

ཤ།

Beef
ḷang-sha

གླང་ཤ།

Chicken
·sha

ཇ་ཤ།

Dried meat
sha kam-po ཤ་སྐམ་པོ།

Fried meat
sha ngos-ma ཤ་བརྫོས་མ།

Fish
nya-sha ཉ་ཤ།

Kidney
khel-ma ཁལ་མ།

Liver
chhin-pa མཆིན་པ།

Mutton (sheep)
lug-sha ལུག་ཤ།

Mutton (goat)
ra-sha ར་ཤ།

Pork
phag-sha ཕག་ཤ།

Sausage
gyu-ma རྒྱུ་མ།

Vegetables
tssel ཚལ །

Cabbage
lo-kho pe-tssel ལོག་འཁོར་པད་ཚལ།

Carrot
go-nga la-phug

སྐྱོང་ལ་ཕུག

Cauliflower
me-tok pe-tssel

མེ་ཏོག་པད་ཚལ།

Chilli
si-pen

སེ་པན།

Green bean
tre-ma

སྒྲན་མ།

Green pepper
si-pen jang-khu

སེ་པན་ལྗང་ཁུ།

Lettuce
pe-tssel

པད་ཚལ།

Onion
tsong

ཙོང་།

Potato
shhog-khog

ཞོ་ཁོག

Radish
la-phug

ལ་ཕུག

Spice
men-na

སྨན་སྣ།

Tomato
to-ma-to

ཀྲོ་མ་ཀྲོ།

Ginger
gog-pa ཨློག་པ།

Cereals
dru-rig འབྲུ་རིགས།

Barley
nes ནས།

Flour
dro-shhib གྲོ་ཞིབ།

Lentils
sen-chhung སྲན་ཆུང་།

Maize
ma-ken ཨ་མོམ།

Rice
dre འབྲས།

Wheat
dro གྲོ།

Fruits
shing-tog ཤིང་ཏོག

Apple
ku-shu ཀུ་ཤུ།

Apricot
<u>ng</u>a-ri kham-bhu མངའ་རིས་ཁམ་བུ།

Banana
ke-la
ཀེ་ལ།

Coconut
be-ta
བེ་ཊ།

Dates
kha-sur
ཁ་སུར།

Mango
am
ཨམ།

Peach
kham-bu
ཁམ་བུ།

Pear
li
ལི།

Pomegranate
siu
སེའུ།

Drinks
thung-rig
འཐུང་རིགས།

Alcohol
a-rak
ཨ་རག

Black tea
tssa-ja
ཚ་ཇ།

Cold drinks
chhu drang-mo
ཆུ་གྲང་མོ།

Milk
wo-ma ཚོ་མ།

Tea
ja ཇ།

Water
chhu ཆུ།

Materials
gyu-chha རྒྱུ་ཆ།

Aluminium
ha-yang ཧ་ཡང་།

Brass
rak རག

Bronze
li-ma ལི་མ།

Ceramics
za-chhes རྫ་ཆས།

Copper
szang ཟངས།

Coral
ju-ru བྱུ་རུ།

Cotton
trin-bel སྤྲིན་བལ།

87

Crystal

shel-szug ཤེལ་གཟུགས།

Fur

tssa-ru ཚ་རུ།

Glass

shel ཤེལ།

Gold

ser གསེར།

Iron

chag ལྕགས།

Ivory

ba-so བ་སོ།

Jade

zul ཇུལ།

Leather

ko-wa ཀོ་བ།

Magnet

ngar-chag དར་ལྕགས།

Metal

chag-rig ལྕགས་རིགས།

Onyx

szi གཟི།

Paper

shu-gu ཤོག་གུ།

88

Pearl
mu-tig ཨུ་ཏིག

Rubber
gyig འགྱིག

Silk
gos-chen གོས་ཆེན།

Silver
ngul དངུལ།

Steel
dhang-chag དྲང་ལྕགས།

Stone
dho རྡོ།

Torquoise
yu གཡུ།

Wood
shing ཤིང་།

Wool
bel བལ།

Stores & services
tssong-khang ཚོང་ཁང་།

Antique
na-ngos གནའ་དངོས་ཚོང་ཁང་།

Bakery
bag-leb བག་ལེབ་ཚོང་ཁང་།

89

Bank

ngul-khang

དངུལ་ཁང་།

Bar

chhang-khang

ཆང་ཁང་།

Barber

tra-shhar-khen

སྐྲ་བཞར་མཁན།

Bookshop

dheb tssong-khang

དེབ་ཚོང་ཁང་།

Clothing store

dhug-log tssong-khang

དུག་སློག

Cobbler

ham szo-khen

ཧམ་བཟོ་མཁན།

Electrician

log szo-khen

གློག་བཟོ་མཁན།

Fruit store

shing-tog tssong-khang

ཤིང་ཏོག་ཚོང་ཁང་།

Grocery

tssel tssong-khang

ཚལ་ཚོང་ཁང་།

Jewellery store

gyen-chha tssong-khang

རྒྱན་ཆ་ཚོང་ཁང་།

Laundary

thran-thru gyab-khen

གོས་ཁྲུས་མཁན།

Liquor shop

a-rak tssong-khang

ཨ་རག་ཚོང་ཁང་།

Market
throm བྲོམ།

Musical instrument store
rol-chha tssong-khang རོལ་ཆ་ཚོང་ཁང་།

Newstand
tssag-pa tsong-sa ཚགས་པར་ཚོང་སཁན།

Shoe store
ham tssong-khang ཧམ་ཚོང་ཁང་།

Tailor
tssem szo-wa ཚེམ་བཟོ་བ།

Toy shop
tse-chhes tsong-khang ཙེད་ཆས་ཚོང་ཁང་།

Watch maker
chhu-tssodh szo-khen ཆུ་ཚོད་བཟོ་མཁན།

Numbers
ang-drang ཨང་གྲངས།

Addition
dhom-tsis བསྡོམས་རྩིས།

Subtraction
then-tsis འཐེན་རྩིས།

Division
gos-tsis བགོས་རྩིས།

Multiplication
gyur-tsis བསྒྱུར་རྩིས།

91

0
le-kor ཀླད་ཀོར།

1
chig གཅིག

2
nyi གཉིས།

3
sum གསུམ།

4
shhi བཞི།

5
nga ལྔ།

6
druk དྲུག

7
dhun བདུན།

8
gye བརྒྱད།

9
gu དགུ།

10
chu བཅུ།

20
nyi-shu ཉི་ཤུ།

21
nyi-shu tsa-chig
ཉི་ཤུ་ཙ་གཅིག

22
nyi-shu tsa-nyi
ཉི་ཤུ་ཙ་གཉིས།

23
nyi-shu tsa sum
ཉི་ཤུ་ཙ་གསུམ།

24
nyi-shu tsa-shhi
ཉི་ཤུ་ཙ་བཞི།

30
sum-chu
སུམ་ཅུ།

35
sum-chu so-nga
སུམ་ཅུ་སོ་ལྔ།

36
sum-chu so-druk
སུམ་ཅུ་སོ་དྲུག

37
sum-chu so-dhun
སུམ་ཅུ་སོ་བདུན།

40
shhi-chu
བཞི་བཅུ།

48
shhi-chu shhe-gye
ཞི་བཅུ་ཞེ་བརྒྱད།

49
shhi-chu shhe-gu
བཞི་བཅུ་ཞེ་དགུ།

50
nga-chu
ལྔ་བཅུ།

60
druk-chu ཊྲུག་བཅུ།

70
dhun-chu བདུན་བཅུ།

80
gye-chu བརྒྱད་བཅུ།

90
gu-chu དགུ་བཅུ།

100
gya བརྒྱ།

200
nyi-gya ཉིས་བརྒྱ།

300
sum-gya སུམ་བརྒྱ།

500
nga-gya ལྔ་བརྒྱ།

1000
chig-tong གཅིག་སྟོང་།

50000
nga-thri ལྔ་ཁྲི།

600000
druk-bum ཊྲུག་འབུམ།

8000000
sa-ya gye ས་ཡ་བརྒྱད།

94

10
Health

Dialogue-I

How are you?
khye-rang dhe-po yin-pey.

ཁྱེད་རང་བདེ་པོ་ཨིན་པས།

I am fine.Thank you.
dhe-po yin. thuk-je-chhe.

བདེ་པོ་ཨིན། ཐུགས་རྗེ་ཆེ།

I don't feel well.
dhe-po min-dhug.

ང་བདེ་པོ་མིན་འདུག

I have a slight headache.
go tog-tsam na-gi dhug.

མགོ་དོག་ཙམ་ན་གི་འདུག

What happened?
ga-re je-song.

ག་རེ་བྱུས་སོང་།

I couldn't sleep last night.
dhang-gong nyi-khug ma-song.

མདང་དགོང་གཉིད་ཁུག་མ་སོང་།

You should see the doctor.
khye-rang em-ji-la ton-go rey.

ཁྱེད་རང་ཨེམ་ཆི་ལ་སྟོན་དགོས་རེད།

I am seeing Dr.Dhondup at 10 a.m. tomorrow.
chhu-tssodh chu-pa-la em-ji dhon-drub thug-ye yin.

ཆུ་ཚོད་བཅུ་པ་ལ་ཨེམ་ཆི་དོན་གྲུབ་ཐུག་ཡི་ཨིན།

95

You are running high fever.

khye-rang la tssa-wa chhen-po dhug.

ཁྱེད་རང་ལ་ཚ་བ་ཆེན་པོ་འདུག

Take this pill every 6 hours.

men dhi chhu-tssodh druk-re-la re-re sza.

སྨན་འདི་ཆུ་ཚོད་དྲུག་རེ་ལ་རེ་རེ་བཟའ།

Dialogue-II

Are you alright?

ga-dre dhug.

ག་འདྲས་འདུག

I have sprained my ankle.

nge kang-pey tssig-chus song.

ངའི་རྐང་པའི་ཚིགས་འཆུས་སོང་།

I have broken my leg.

ngay kang-pa chhag-song.

ངའི་རྐང་པ་ཆག་སོང་།

I hurt my head.

ngey go dhab-song.

ངའི་མགོ་བརྡབས་སོང་།

Take him to the hospital.

men-khang thri-gyug.

ཁོ་སྨན་ཁང་འཁྲིད་རྒྱུགས།

Call the ambulance.

men-khang mo-tra ke-tang

སྨན་ཁང་མོ་ཊ་སྐད་གཏོང་།

Is he breathing?

kho ug tang-gi dhug-ge.

ཁོ་དབུགས་གཏོང་གི་འདུག་གས།

It is an emergency.

dhi za-drag-po dhug.

འདི་ཟ་དྲགས་པོ་འདུག

96

Get a stretcher.

mi khyer-sa chig khyer-shog.

མི་འཁྱེར་ས་ཞིག་ཁྲི་གཅིག་འཁྱེར་ཤོག

Carry him on your back.

kho khye-rang gi gel-par khyer-rog.

ཁོ་ཁྱེད་རང་གི་སྒལ་པར་འཁྱེར་རོགས།

Don't worry.

sem-threl ma-nang.

སེམས་ཁྲལ་མ་གནང་།

Dialogue-III

Are you ill?

na-gi dhug-ge.

ན་ཡི་འདུག་གས།

I have tuberculosis.

ti-bi na-gi dhug.

ཏེ་བི་ན་ཡི་འདུག

Aren't you staying at the hospital.

men-khang-la dhe-gi me-pey.

སྨན་ཁང་ལ་སྡོད་ཀྱི་མེད་པས།

I just came to buy some fruits.

nga shing-tog nyo-la yong-wa yin.

ང་ཤིང་ཏོག་ཉོ་ལ་ཡོང་བ་ཡིན།

You should eat well.

kha-lag yag-po sza-go rey.

ཁ་ལག་ཡག་པོ་བཟའ་དགོས་རེད།

It is so boring to eat so many medicines.

men mang-po sza-ye nyop-to shhe-po dhug.

སྨན་མང་པོ་བཟའ་ཡི་ནོ་པོ་ཞེ་དྲག་འདུག

Don't you also have to take many injections?

khab mang-po gyab-go ma-re pey.

ཁབ་མང་པོ་རྒྱག་དགོས་མ་རེད་པས།

97

Twice every day.
nyi-ma chig-la theng-nyi.
ཉི་མ་གཅིག་ལ་ཐེངས་གཉིས།

It must be difficult.
ka-les khag-po yo-gi-rey.
དཀའ་ལས་ཁག་པོ་ཡོད་ཀྱི་རེད།

I love it.
kyi-po dhug.
སྐྱིད་པོ་འདུག

Dialogue-IV

What happened?
ga-re je-song
ག་རེ་བྱུས་སོང་།

There has been a car accident.
mo-tra dhab-shag.
མོ་ཊ་བརྡབས་ཤག

Did anybody die?
mi shi dhug-ge.
མི་ཤི་འདུག་གས།

No. Fortunately.
min-dhug. tab yag-ga-la.
མིན་འདུག སྟབས་ཡག་ག་ལ།

The driver's leg is broken.
mo-tra tong-khen kang-pa chhag-shhag.
མོ་ཊ་གཏོང་མཁན་རྐང་པ་ཆག་ཤག

Who else are with him?
shhen su-dhug.
ཤོ་མཉམ་དུ་གཞན་སུ་འདུག

There is a mother and a child in the back seat.
gyab-la a-ma chig-dhang thru-gu chig-dhug.
རྒྱབ་ལ་ཨ་མ་གཅིག་དང་ཕྲུ་གུ་གཅིག་འདུག

98

The mother is unconscious.
a-ma dhi dren-pa thhor-shhag.

ཨ་མ་འདི་དྲན་པ་ཐོར་ཤག

The child is okay.
thru-gu thhang-thhang re-shhag.

ཕྲུ་གུ་ཐང་ཐང་རེད་ཤག

Try to relax.
lhodh-lhodh nang.

ལྷོད་ལྷོད་གནང་།

VOCABULARY-I

Appetite
dhang-ga

དང་ག

Asthma
ug-sag na-tssa

དབུགས་བསགས་ན་ཚ།

Allergic
ma-thros-pa

མ་འཕྲོས་པ།

Boil
nyen-bur

རྙན་འབུར།

Blood
thrag

ཁྲག

Blood pressure
thrag-shedh

ཁྲག་ཤེད།

Bandages
ma-tri

མ་དཀྲིས།

99

Bleeding
thrag-thon ཁྲག་ཐོན།

Cholera
shel-kyug བཤལ་སྐྱུག

Cold
chham-pa འཆམ་པ།

Cough
lo གློ།

Cotton wool
trin-bel སྤྲིན་བལ།

Cavity
khog-tong ཁོག་སྟོང་།

Dentist
so em-ji སོ་ཨེམ་ཆི།

Diarrhoea
shel-ne བཤལ་ནད།

Denture
so-tssab སོ་ཚབ།

Epidemic
ne-yam ནད་ཡམས།

Eye drops
mig-men མིག་སྨན།

Fever
tssa-wa ཚ་བ།

Fracture
chhag-drum ཆག་གྲུམ།

Food poisoning
sze-dhug ཟས་དུག

headache
go-ne མགོ་ནད།

Jaundice
thri-pa མཁྲིས་པ།

Medicine
men སྨན།

Measles
si-bi སི་བི།

Nose bleeding
na-thrag སྣ་ཁྲག

Ointment
juk-men བྱུག་སྨན།

Pain
na-tssa ན་ཚ།

Pus
nag རྣག

101

Sore throat

mig-pey na-tssa

མིད་པའི་ན་ཚ།

Swell

trang-wa

སྐྲང་བ།

Sprain

tssig chhus-pa

ཚིགས་འཆུས་པ།

Surgeon

shag-chos em-ji

གཤག་བཅོས་ཨེམ་ཆི།

Toothache

so na-wa

སོ་ན་བ།

Temperature

tssa-wa

ཚ་བ།

Thermometer

tssa-wa ta-chhe

ཚ་བ་ལྟ་ཆས།

Vomit

kyug-pa

སྐྱུག་པ།

VOCABULARY-II

Parts of the body

lus-gi chha-shes

ལུས་ཀྱི་ཆ་ཤས།

Abdomen

dro-khog

གྲོད་ཁོག

Ankle

bol-gong

བོལ་གོང་།

Arm
lag-ngar

ལག་དར།

Armpit
chhen-gung

མཆན་གུང་།

Back
todh-gel

སྟོད་རྒྱལ།

Backbone
gel-tssig

རྒྱལ་ཚིགས།

Belly
to-wa

གྲོད་བ།

Blood
thrag

ཁྲག

Body
szug-po

གཟུགས་པོ།

Bone
ru-gog

རུས་གོག

Brain
le-pa

ཀླད་པ།

Breast
nu-ma

ནུ་མ།

Calf
nyab-ril

ཉ་རིལ།

Cheek
khur-tssos

མཁུར་ཚོས།

103

Chest
drang-khog
ब्रद'वॅन

Chin
ma-li
अ'थे|

Collarbone
jing-tssig
अङिद'क्षेनाक्ष|

Ear
am-chog
जुअ'र्डेन

Earlobe
na-shel
ब्रु'यल|

Elbow
dru-mo
ग्रु'र्सी|

Eye
<u>mig</u>
अेन

Eyebrow
<u>mig</u>-szi
अेन'नाड़े|

Eyelid
<u>mig</u>-pag
अेन'ब्लनाक्ष|

Eyelash
<u>mig</u>-pu
अेन'ब्लु|

Face
dhong
नार्देद'|

Finger
zu-gu
अङ्डैव'र्सी|

104

Finger nail
sen-mo
སེན་མོ།

Foot/feet
kang-pa
རྐང་པ།

Gums
so-sha
སོ་ཤ།

Hair(head)
tra
སྐྲ།

Hair (body)
pu
སྤུ།

Hand
lag-pa
ལག་པ།

Heart
nying
སྙིང་།

Heel
ting-ga
རྟིང་པ།

Hip
chi-go
དཔྱི་མགོ།

Jaw
dram-pa
འགྲམ་པ།

Knee
pi-mo
པུས་མོ།

Leg
kang-pa
རྐང་པ།

Lip
chhu-to
མཆུ་ཏོ།

Mouth
kha
ཁ།

Navel
te-wa
ལྟེ་བ།

Nose
na-gu
སྣ།

Nostril
na-khung
སྣ་ཁུང་།

Palm
lag-thil
ལག་མཐིལ།

Rib
tsig-ma
རྩིབས་མ།

Shoulder
pung-pa
དཔུང་པ།

Skin
pag-pa
པགས་པ།

Skull
kab-li
ཀ་པ་ལི།

Sole
kang-thil
རྐང་མཐིལ།

Stomach
dro-khog
གྲོད་ཁོག

Temple

yar-khung ཡ་ཁུང་།

Thigh

la-sha བརྫ་ཤ།

Throat

mig-pa མིད་པ།

thumb

thhe-wo མཐེ་བོང་།

Tongue

che-le ཅེ།

Waist

kye-pa སྐེད་པ།

Wrist

lag-tssig ལག་ཚིགས།

11

Room hunting

Dialogue-I

Do you know where I can find a room?
nes-tssang yar-sa ga-wa ra-gi rey.

གནས་ཚང་གཡར་ས་ག་པར་རག་གི་རེད།

Go to Hotel Tibet.
bodh-gi dron-khang-la gyug.

བོད་ཀྱི་མགྲོན་ཁང་ལ་རྒྱུགས།

Where is it?
ga-wa yo-rey.

ག་པར་ཡོད་རེད།

It is near the bus stand.
bas ti-sing dram yo-rey.

རྩངས་འབོར་འབབ་ཚུགས་འགྲམ་ཡོད་རེད།

Is this Hotel Tibet?
dhi bodh-gi dron-khang re-pey.

འདི་བོད་ཀྱི་མགྲོན་ཁང་རེད་པས།

Are there any vacant rooms?
dhey-la khang-mig tong-pa yo-re-pey.

དེ་ལ་ཁང་མིག་སྟོང་པ་ཡོད་རེད་པས།

Yes.
yo-rey.

ཡོད་རེད།

Do you want a double room?
khye-rang la mi-nyi nyel-khang go-pey.

ཁྱེད་རང་ལ་མི་གཉིས་ཉལ་ཁང་དགོས་པས།

108

I want a single room.
nga-la mi-chig nyel-khang go.

ང་ལ་མི་གཅིག་ཉལ་ཁང་དགོས།

How much is the room rent?
khang-la ga-tssodh rey.

ཁང་ལྐ་ག་ཚོད་རེད།

It is Rs.450 per day.
nyin-rer gor shhi-gya nga-chu rey.

ཉིན་རེར་སྒོར་བཞི་བརྒྱ་ལྔ་བཅུ་རེད།

That is too expensive.
gong chhe-dra-shhag.

གོང་ཆེ་དྲག་ཞག

Sorry. We don't have any cheaper rooms.
gon-dhag. nga-tssor dhi-les gong khe-wey khang-pa mey.

དགོངས་དག ང་ཚོར་འདི་ལས་ཁེ་བའི་ཁང་པ་མེད།

Where can I find cheaper rooms?
khang-mig khe-wa ga-wa ra-gi rey.

ཁང་པ་ཁེ་བ་ག་པར་རག་གི་རེད།

Go to Shangrila hotel.
shang-ri-la dron-khang-la.

ཞང་རི་ལ་མགྲོན་ཁང་ལ།

Dialogue-II

Are there any vacant rooms?
khang-pa tong-pa yo-pey.

ཁང་པ་སྟོང་པ་ཡོད་པས།

We have two vacant rooms.
khang-mig tong-pa nyi-yodh.

ཁང་མིག་སྟོང་པ་གཉིས་ཡོད།

How much is the rent?
khang-la ga-tssodh rey.

ཁང་ལྐ་ག་ཚོད་རེད།

Rs.150 per day.
nyin-rer gor gya-dhang nga-chu rey.

ཉིན་རེར་སྒོར་བརྒྱ་དང་ལྔ་བཅུ།

Can I see the room?
khang-pa ta-na drig-gi re-pey.

ཁང་པ་བལྟ་ན་འགྲིག་གི་རེད་པས།

I will take the room.
khang-mig dhi len-gi yin.

ཁང་མིག་འདི་ལེན་གྱི་ཡིན།

Please fill in this form.
geng-shog dhi gyang-rog nang.

འགེངས་ཤོག་འདི་རྒྱངས་རོགས་གནང་།

Sign here, please.
dhey-la tssen-tag kyon-rog nang.

དེ་ལ་མཚན་རྟགས་བསྐྱོན་རོགས་གནང་།

How long will you be staying?
khye-rang nyi-ma ga-tssodh shhug-ye yin.

ཁྱེད་རང་ཉི་མ་ག་ཚོད་བཞུགས་ཡེ་ཡིན།

For a month.
dha-wa chig.

ཟླ་བ་གཅིག

What is my room number?
ngey khang-mig ang-drang ga-tssodh rey.

ངའི་ཁང་མིག་ཨང་གྲངས་ག་ཚོད་རེད།

It is 101.
gya-dhang-chig rey.

བརྒྱ་དང་གཅིག་རེད།

Do you want someone to carry your bags?
khye-rang gi cha-lag khyer-gen go-pey.

ཁྱེད་རང་གི་ཅ་ལག་འཁྱེར་མཁན་དགོས་པས།

No. I will carry it.
mo-gos. nga-rang khyer-gi-yin.

མི་དགོས། ང་རང་འཁྱེར་གྱི་ཡིན།

110

Can I have the keys of my room?
ngey khang-mig gi dhe-mig tre-rog nang.

ངའི་ཁང་མིག་གི་ལྡེ་མིག་སྤྲད་རོགས་གནང་།

Here they are.
dhe-mig dhey-la yodh.

ལྡེ་མིག་དེ་ལ་ཡོད།

Dialogue-III

Can you help me find a place to stay?
nga-la nes-tssang yar-sa chig tssel-rog nang.

ང་ལ་གནས་ཚང་གཡར་ས་གཅིག་འཚོལ་རོགས་གནང་།

There are so many hotels here.
dhey-la dron-khang mang-po yo-rey.

དེ་ལ་མགྲོན་ཁང་མང་པོ་ཡོད་རེད།

I don't want to stay in a hotel.
nga dron-khang nang dhe-dhodh mey.

ང་མགྲོན་ཁང་ནང་བསྡད་འདོད་མེད།

Why?
ga-re je-nes.

ག་རེ་བྱས་ནས།

I plan to stay here for a year.
dhey-la lo-chig dhe-tsis yodh.

དེ་ལ་ལོ་གཅིག་བསྡད་རྩིས་ཡོད།

Doing what?
ga-re je-tsis yodh.

ག་རེ་བྱེད་རྩིས་ཡོད།

I want to study Buddhism.
nang-chhos jang-ye yodh.

ནང་ཆོས་སྦྱང་ཡི་ཡིན།

You should stay in the villages.
khye-rang drong-seb nang-la dhe go-rey.

ཁྱེད་རང་གྲོང་གསེབ་ནང་ལ་བསྡད་དགོས་རེད།

111

Are they safe?
drong-seb ten-po yo-re-pey.

གྲོང་གསེབ་བརྟན་པོ་ཡོད་རེད་པས།

Yes and they are cheap too.
yo-rey. gong-yang khe-po yo-rey.

ཡོད་རེད། གོང་ཡང་ཁེ་པོ་ཡོད་རེད།

I want to stay near the Tibetan library.
nga pe-zodh-khang dram-la dhe-dhodh yodh.

ང་དཔེ་མཛོད་ཁང་འགྲམ་ལ་བསྡད་འདོད་ཡོད།

There are families who rent out rooms.
nang-mi kha-shes so-sos ger-gi khang-pa yar-gi rey.

ནང་མི་ཁ་ཤས་སོ་སོས་སྐྱེར་གྱི་ཁང་པ་གཡར་གྱི་རེད།

I will stay in one of them.
nga dhey-dre khang-pa chig-nang dhe-gi yin.

ང་དེ་གྲས་ཁང་པ་གཅིག་ནང་བསྡད་ཀྱི་ཡིན།

Will they reduce the rent if I stay for a year?
lo-chig dhe-na khang-la chag-gi re-pey.

ལོ་གཅིག་བསྡད་ན་ཁང་ལྷ་གཆག་གི་རེད་པས།

I don't know. Maybe.
ha-go ma-song. chig-je-na chag sidh-pa rey.

ཧ་གོ་མ་སོང་། གཅིག་བྱས་ན་གཆག་སྲིད་པ་རེད།

Dialogue-IV

Where is the hotel manager's office?
dron-khang gi gen-zin ga-wa yo-rey.

མགྲོན་ཁང་གི་འགན་འཛིན་ག་པར་ཡོད་རེད།

Why?
ga-re je-song.

ག་རེ་བྱས་སོང་།

I have to speak to him.
khos-nyam ke-cha she-go yodh.

ཁོས་མཉམ་སྐད་ཆ་བཤད་དགོས་ཡོད།

You can register your complaints here.
sam-chhar yodh-na dhey-la lab-na drig-gi rey.

བསམ་འཆར་ཡོད་ན་དེ་ལ་ལབ་ན་འགྲིག་གི་རེད།

The fan in my room is not working.
ngey khang-mig gi lung-khor dro-gi mi-dhug.

ངའི་ཁང་མིག་གི་རླུང་འཁོར་འགྲོ་ཡི་མི་འདུག

The common toilets are very dirty.
sang-chodh zor-po shhe-po dhug.

གསང་སྤྱོད་མཛོར་པོ་ཞེ་པོ་འདུག

I need more blankets.
nga-la nyel-chhe kha-shes go.

ང་ལ་ཉལ་ཆས་ཁ་ཤས་དགོས།

There is no towel in my bathroom.
ngey thru-khang nang-la a-chor min-dhug.

ངའི་འཁྲུས་ཁང་ནང་ལ་ཨ་ཆོར་མིན་འདུག

Can I leave my room keys here.
ngey khang-mig-gi dhe-mig dhey-la shhag-na drig-gi re-pey.

ངའི་ཁང་མིག་གི་ལྡེ་མིག་དེ་ལ་བཞག་ན་འགྲིག་གི་རེད་པས།

When is check-out time?
ga-dhus thon-go rey.

ག་དུས་འཐོན་དགོས་རེད།

Checkout time is 12 noon.
nyin-gung chhu-tssodh chu-nyi-la thon-go rey.

ཉིན་གུང་ཆུ་ཚོད་བཅུ་གཉིས་ལ་འཐོན་དགོས་རེད།

I want to shift to another room.
nga khang-mig shhen-la po-gi yin.

ང་ཁང་མིག་གཞན་ལ་སྤོ་ཡི་ཡིན།

Where is the landlord?
khang-dhag ga-wa chhin-song.

ཁང་བདག་ག་པར་ཕྱིན་སོང་།

Can I pay my room rent next month?
khang-la dha-wa je-ma tre-na drig-gi re-pey.

ཁང་གླ་ཟླ་བ་རྗེས་མ་སྤྲད་ན་འགྲིག་གི་རེད་པས།

113

I will pay six months room rent in advance.
dha-wa druk-gi khang-la ngon-la tre-gi yin

ཟླ་བ་དྲུག་གི་ཁང་ལ་སྔ་སྔོན་ལ་སྤྲད་ཀྱི་ཡིན།

VOCABULARY

Advance
nga-dhon

སྔ་འདོན།

Bag
to-phe

སྦོ་ཕད།

Bed
nyel-thri

ཉལ་ཁྲི།

Cheap
gong khe-wa

གོང་ཁེ་བ།

Checkout time
thon-ye dhus-tssodh

འཐོན་ཡི་དུས་ཚོད།

Clean
tsang-ma

གཙང་མ།

Complaint
sam-chhar

བསམ་འཆར།

Dirty
zor-po

མཛོར་པོ།

Double
mi-nyi nyel-sa

མི་གཉིས་ཉལ་ས།

114

Expensive
gong chhen-po

གོང་ཆེན་པོ།

Fan
lung-khor

རླུང་འཁོར།

Form
geng-shog

འགེངས་ཤོག

Help
rog-pa

རོགས་པ།

Hotei
dron-khang

མགྲོན་ཁང་།

Key
dhe-mig

ལྡེ་མིག

Landlord
khang-dhag

ཁང་བདག

Lock
go-chag

སྒོ་ལྕགས།

Luggage
cha-lag

ཅ་ལག

Manager
gen-zin

འགན་འཛིན།

Office
yig-tssang

ཡིག་ཚང་།

Private
ger སྒེར།

Pillow
ngel-go སྔས་མགོ།

Reduce
gong chag-pa གོང་བཅག་པ།

Rent
khang-la ཁང་གླ།

Room
khang-mig ཁང་མིག

Single
mi-chig nyel-sa མི་གཅིག་ཉལ་ས།

Signature
tssen-tag མཚན་རྟགས།

Stay
dhe-pa བསྡད་པ།

Shift
po-wa སྤོ་བ།

Towel
a-chor ཨ་ཆོར།

Vacant
tong-pa སྟོང་པ།

12
Travelling

Dialogue-I

I am taking a two months leave.
nga dha-wa nyi gong-pa len-ye yin.

ང་ཟླ་བ་གཉིས་དགོངས་པ་ལེན་ཡི་ཡིན།

Why?
ga-re je-nes.

ག་རེ་བྱས་ནས།

I have to go to India.
nga gya-gar-la dro-go yodh.

ང་རྒྱ་གར་ལ་འགྲོ་དགོས་ཡོད།

To do what?
ga-re je-ga.

ག་རེ་བྱེད་ག

I want to study Buddhism.
nang-chos jang-ye yin.

ནང་ཆོས་སྦྱང་ཡི་ཡིན།

Have you booked your air tickets?
nam-dru tri-ka-si nyo-tssar yin-pey.

གནམ་གྲུ་ཊི་ཀ་སི་ཉོས་ཚར་ཡིན་པེ།

I plan to do it today.
dhey-ring nyo-tsis yodh.

དེ་རིང་ཉོས་རྩིས་ཡོད།

I need an economy class ticket to Delhi.
dhi-li bar-dhu nam-dru tri-ka-si gong khe-wa chig nang-rog.

དི་ལི་བར་དུ་གནམ་གྲུ་ཊི་ཀ་སི་གོང་ཁེ་བ་གཅིག་གནང་རོགས།

117

That will be $500

dro-lar nga-gya rey.

གྲོ་ལར་ལྔ་བརྒྱ་རེད།

We will make the necessary arrangements.

nga-tssos dra-drig je-chhog.

ང་ཚོས་གྲ་སྒྲིག་བྱེད་མ་ཆོག

When do you plan to leave?

ga-dhus thon-chhar yodh.

ག་དུས་ཐོན་འཆར་ཡོད།

Next Friday.

dhun-thrag je-mey sza pa-sang.

བདུན་ཕྲག་རྗེས་མའི་གཟའ་པ་སངས།

Don't carry any excess baggage.

cha-lag mang-po ma-khyer.

ཅ་ལག་མང་པོ་མ་འཁྱེར།

I always travel light.

nga ga-dhus yi-nay cha-lag mang-po khyer-gi mey.

ང་ག་དུས་ཡིན་ནའི་ཅ་ལག་མང་པོ་འཁྱེར་གྱི་མེད།

How long will the air journey take?

nam-dru nang-la chhu-tssodh ga-tssodh dro-go rey.

གནམ་གྲུ་ནང་ལ་ཆུ་ཚོད་ག་ཚོད་འགྲོ་དགོས་རེད།

About 24 hours.

chhu-tssodh nyi-shu tsa-shhi tsam dro-go rey.

ཆུ་ཚོད་ཉི་ཤུ་རྩ་བཞི་ཙམ་འགྲོ་དགོས་རེད།

Have a nice journey.

ga-le pheb-go.

ག་ལེ་ཕེབས་གོ།

Farewell

gyog-po jel-yong.

མགྱོགས་པོ་མཇལ་ཡོང་།

Dialogue-II

Are you visitig India for the first time?
khye-rang gya-gar-la yong-wa theng-ma dhang-po yin-pey.

ཁྱེད་རང་རྒྱ་གར་ལ་ཡོང་བ་ཐེངས་དང་པོ་ཡིན་པས།

Yes.
la-wong.

ལ་འོང་།

Where do you plan to go?
gya-gar sa-cha ga-wa-la dro-tsis yodh.

རྒྱ་གར་ས་ཆ་ག་པར་ལ་འགྲོ་རྩིས་ཡོད།

Dharamsala.
dha-ram-sa-la

དྷ་རམ་ས་ལ།

For what purpose?
les-dhon ga-re yin-na.

ལས་དོན་ག་རེ་ཡིན་ན།

Study.
lob-jong.

སློབ་སྦྱོང་།

Can we have a look at your passport?
khye-rang gi pa-si ton-rog nang.

ཁྱེད་རང་གི་པ་སི་སྟོན་རོགས་གནང་།

Of course.
yin-dha-yin.

ཡིན་ད་ཡིན།

You may go now.
khye-rang dro-na drig-gi rey.

ཁྱེད་རང་འགྲོ་ན་འགྲིག་གི་རེད།

Where can I get a taxi?
trek-si[26] ga-wa ra-gi rey.

མོ་ཊ་ག་པར་རག་གི་རེད།

---

26. Trek-si is a corruption of the word taxi.

At the back of this building.

thog-tseg dhi gyab-la.

ཐོག་རྩེག་འདིའི་རྒྱབ་ལ།

How much to the Imperial hotel.

dron-khang bar-dhu gong ga-tssodh rey.

མགྲོན་ཁང་བར་དུ་གོང་ག་ཚོད་རེད།

We will go by the meter.

nga-tsso mi-tar shhir-szung dro-go.

ང་ཚོ་མི་ཊར་གཞིར་བཟུང་འགྲོ་གོ།

As you wish.

khye-rang thug-mos tar.

ཁྱེད་རང་ཐུགས་མོས་ལྟར།

Here is the Imperial hotel.

dron-khang-la leb-song.

མགྲོན་ཁང་ལ་སླེབས་སོང་།

I have booked a room for two days.

ngey ming-thog-la nyin-nyi ring khang-pa le-yodh.

ངའི་མིང་ཐོག་ལ་ཉིན་གཉིས་རིང་ཁང་པ་བླས་ཡོད།

Sir, what is your name?

khye-rang gi tssen ga-re yin-na.

ཁྱེད་རང་གི་མཚན་ག་རེ་ཡིན་ན།

Jack.

jek.

ཇེཀ།

Sign here, please.

dhey-la tssen-tag kyon-rog nang.

དེ་ལ་མཚན་རྟགས་བསྐྱོན་རོགས་གནང་།

Dialogue-III

I have to go to Dharamsala.

nga dha-ram-sa-lar dro-go yodh.

ང་དྷ་རམ་ས་ལར་འགྲོ་དགོས་ཡོད།

Is there a train to Dharamsala?

dha-sa bar ri-li yo-re-pey.

དྷ་ས་བར་རི་ལི་ཡོད་རེད་པས།

There is but it does not go all the way to Dharamsala.

yo-rey. yi-nay ri-li dhi dha-sa bar tag-tag kyel-gi ma-rey.

ཡོད་རེད། ཡིན་ནའི་རི་ལི་འདི་དྷ་ས་བར་ཏག་ཏག་བསྐྱེལ་གྱི་མ་རེད།

So?

a-ni.

ཨ་ནི།

It goes to Pathankot.

ri-li dhi pa-than-kot bar-dhu dro-gi rey.

རི་ལི་འདི་པ་ཏན་ཀོཊ་བར་འགྲོ་ཡི་རེད།

From there you will have to take a bus to Dharamsala.

dhi-nes khye-rang dha-sa bar ba-si nang dro go-gi rey.

འདི་ནས་ཁྱེད་རང་དྷ་ས་བར་བ་སི་ནང་འགྲོ་དགོས་ཀྱི་རེད།

How far is Dharamsala from Pathankot?

dha-sa nes Pa-than-kot bar thag-ring-los yo-rey.

དྷ་ས་ནས་པ་ཏན་ཀོཊ་བར་ཐག་རིང་ལོས་ཡོད་རེད།

About four hours ride by bus.

bas nang dro-na chhu-tssodh shhi-rey.

བ་སི་ནང་འགྲོ་ན་ཆུ་ཚོད་བཞི་རེད།

I think I will take the direct bus.

a-les je-na nga ba-si nang-la the-kar dha-sar dro-na yag-sa rey.

ཨ་ལས་བྱས་ན་ང་བ་སི་ནང་ལ་ཐད་ཀར་དྷ་སར་འགྲོ་ན་ཡག་ས་རེད།

You should take the Potala bus.

khye-rang Po-ta-la ba-si nang dro-na yag-po yo-rey.

ཁྱེད་རང་པོ་ཏ་ལ་བ་སི་ནང་འགྲོ་ན་ཡག་པོ་ཡོད་རེད།

How much is it?

la-cha ga-tssodh rey.

གླ་ཆ་ག་ཚོད་རེད།

Rs.350.

mi-rer gor sum-gya nga-chu.

མི་རེར་སྒོར་སུམ་བརྒྱ་ལྔ་བཅུ།

Isn't that too much?
dhi gong chhen-po ma-re-pey.

འདི་གོང་ཆེན་པོ་མ་རེད་པས།

The price of petrol has gone up.
num gong phar yo-rey.

སྣུམ་གོང་འཕར་ཡོད་རེད།

When does the bus leave?
ba-si ga-dhus thon-gi rey.

བ་སི་ག་དུས་འཐོན་གྱི་རེད།

It leaves at 6.30 p.m.
gon-dhag chhu-tssodh druk dhang chhe-ka.

དགོང་དག་ཆུ་ཚོད་དྲུག་དང་ཕྱེད་ཀ

How long is the bus journey?
ba-si nang yun ring-los dro-go rey.

བ་སི་ནང་ཡུན་རིང་ལོས་འགྲོ་དགོས་རེད།

About 12 hours.
chhu-tssodh chu-nyi tsam.

ཆུ་ཚོད་བཅུ་གཉིས་ཙམ།

Where is seat no.27?
kub-kyag ang-ki nyi-shu tsa-dhun ga-wa rey.

ཀུབ་བཀྱག་ཨང་གྲངས་ཉི་ཤུ་རྩ་བདུན་ག་པར་རེད།

Here. At the back.
dhey. gyab-la.

དེ། རྒྱབ་ལ།

Where will the bus stop?
ba-si dhi ga-wa ka-gi rey.

བ་སི་འདི་ག་པར་བཀག་གི་རེད།

It will stop for sometime at Chandigarh.
chan-dhi-gar-la tog-tssam ka-gi rey.

ཙན་དི་གར་ལ་ཏོག་ཙམ་བཀག་གི་རེད།

For how long?
ga-tssodh ka-gi rey.

ག་ཚོད་བཀག་གི་རེད།

About 30 minutes.
kar-ma sum-chu tsam.

སྐར་མ་སུམ་ཅུ་ཙམ།

Is there a restaurant there?
phi-ge-la sza-khang yo-re-pey.

ཕ་གིར་ཟ་ཁང་ཡོད་རེད་པས།

Yes.
yo-rey.

ཡོད་རེད།

Driver, can you please stop?
ku-chi. ba-si tog-tsam ka-rog nang.

ཀུ་ཅི། བ་སི་ཏོག་ཙམ་བཀག་རོགས་གནང་།

We can't stop in the middle of nowhere.
nga-tsso ga-wa ga-sar ka chhog-gi ma-rey.

ང་ཚོ་ག་བ་གསར་བཀག་མཆོག་གི་མ་རེད།

I have to go to the toilet.
nga chhab-sang-la dro-go yodh.

ང་ཆབ་གསང་ལ་འགྲོ་དགོས་ཡོད།

We will stop at Una for five minutes.
nga-tsso u-nar kar-ma nga-tsam ka-gi rey.

ང་ཚོ་ཨུ་ནར་སྐར་མ་ལྔ་ཙམ་བཀག་གི་རེད།

Where is the toilet?
sang-chodh ga-wa yo-rey.

གསང་སྤྱོད་ག་པར་ཡོད་རེད།

There is no toilet.
dhey-la sang-chodh yo-ma-rey.

དེ་ལ་གསང་སྤྱོད་ཡོད་མ་རེད།

What is the name of that village?
drong-seb pha-gi ming-la ga-re rey.

གྲོང་གསེབ་ཕ་གི་མིང་ལ་ག་རེ་རེད།

Kangra.
kang-ra.

ཀང་ར།

This is Dharamsala.

dha-sar leb-song.

ད་སར་སླེབས་སོང་།

Can you get me a porter?

nga-la ku-li[27] chig tssel-rog nang.

ང་ལ་དོས་འབྲེར་གཅིག་བཙལ་རོགས་གནང་།

Take these luggage to Hotel Tibet.

cha-lag dhi-tsso bodh-gi dron-khang-la khyer-rog.

ཅ་ལག་འདི་ཚོ་བོད་ཀྱི་མགྲོན་ཁང་ལ་འཁྱེར་རོགས།

Dialogue-IV

Where is the hair salon?

tra shhar-sa ga-wa rey.

སྐྲ་བཞར་ས་ག་པར་ཡོད་རེད།

There are two in the next street.

sang-lam phar-chhog nang tra-shhar-sa nyi yo-rey.

སྲང་ལམ་ཕར་ཕྱོགས་ནང་སྐྲ་བཞར་ས་གཉིས་ཡོད་རེད།

How much for a haircut?

tra shhar-la ga-tssodh rey.

སྐྲ་བཞར་སྐྲ་ག་ཚོད་རེད།

Rs. 20.

gor nyi-shu.

སྒོར་ཉི་ཤུ།

Are there any video parlours here?

dhey-la log-nyen ta-sa yo-re-pey.

དེ་ལ་གློག་བརྙན་ལྟ་ས་ཡོད་རེད་པས།

There are two on the way to the post office.

drag-khang dro-sey lam-la log-nyen ta-sa nyi yo-rey.

སྒྲུག་ཁང་འགྲོ་སའི་ལམ་ལ་གློག་བརྙན་ལྟ་ས་གཉིས་ཡོད་རེད།

---

27. Ku-li is a corruption of the Indian word coolie (porters).

Do they show English movies?

in-ji log-nyen ton-gi yo-re-pey.

དབྱིན་ཇི་གློག་བརྙན་སྟོན་གྱི་ཡོད་རེད་པས།

They show the latest Hollywood movies.

in-ji log-nyen sar-pa tssang-ma ton-gi yo-rey.

དབྱིན་ཇི་གློག་བརྙན་གསར་པ་ཚང་མ་སྟོན་གྱི་ཡོད་རེད།

Where can I change dollars?

dro-lar je-sa ga-wa rey.

གྲོ་ལར་བརྗེ་ས་ག་པར་ཡོད་རེད།

Ask that man with the red cap.

mi pha-gi shha-mo mar-po gon-gen dhey-la ke-cha dris.

མི་ཕ་གི་ཞྭ་མོ་དམར་པོ་གྱོན་མཁན་དེ་ལ་སྐད་ཆ་དྲིས།

How much do you give for one dollar?

khye-rang do-lar chig-la ga-tssodh tre-gi yodh.

ཁྱེད་རང་གྲོ་ལར་གཅིག་ལ་ག་ཚོད་སྤྲོད་ཀྱི་ཡོད།

Forty two rupees.

gor shhi-chu shhe-druk.

སྒོར་བཞི་བཅུ་ཞེ་དྲུག

Can I get an audience with H.H. the Dalai Lama?

nga gong-sa-chhog jel chhog-gi re-pey.

ང་༧གོང་ས་མཆོག་མཇལ་མཆོག་གི་རེད་པས།

Register your name at the Security office.

khye-rang dhe-sung les-khung-la ming-tho gyab-go rey.

ཁྱེད་རང་བདེ་སྲུང་ལས་ཁུངས་ལ་མིང་ཐོ་བརྒྱབ་དགོས་རེད།

Where is that?

les-khung dhi ga-wa yo-rey.

ལས་ཁུངས་འདི་ག་པར་ཡོད་རེད།

It is on the road to Bhagsu Nath.

bhag-su Nath dro-sey lam-la yo-rey.

བག་སུ་ནཱཐ་འགྲོ་སའི་ལམ་ལ་ཡོད་རེད།

125

Dialogue-V

I want to make a phone call.
nga kha-par tang-go yodh.
ང་ཁ་པར་གཏང་དགོས་ཡོད།

Where?
ga-wa-la.
ག་པར་ལ།

New York.
a-ri New York.
ཨ་རི་ཉིའུ་ཡོག

Please wait a minute.
kar-ma chig gug-rog nang.
སྐར་མ་གཅིག་སྒུག་རོགས་གནང་།

The line is not very clear.
kha-par sel-po shhe-dra min-dhug.
ཁ་པར་གསལ་པོ་མིན་འདུག

Hello! Who is this speaking?
ha-lo. su yin-pey.
ཧ་ལོ། སུ་ཡིན་པས།

This is Jack speaking.
dhi Jek yin.
འདི་ཇེག་ཡིན།

Can you speak louder?
sung-ke chhe-si kyon-rog nang.
སུང་སྐད་ཆེ་ཙམ་བསྐྱོན་རོགས་གནང་།

I want to speak to my father.
nga pa-la nyam-dhu ke-cha she-go yodh.
ང་པ་ལགས་མཉམ་དུ་སྐད་ཆ་བཤད་དགོས་ཡོད།

He is in the kitchen.
kho-rang thab-tssang nang dhug.
ཁོ་རང་ཐབ་ཚང་ནང་འདུག

Please hold the line. I will call him.
kar-ma chig gug-rog-nang. nge ke tang-go.
སྐར་མ་གཅིག་སྒུག་རོགས་གནང་། ངས་སྐད་གཏང་གོ

126

He went outside.
kho-rang chhi-log-la chhin-shhag.

ཁོ་རང་ཕྱི་ལོག་ལ་ཕྱིན་པས།

Can you call back later?
khye-rang kha-par je-la tang-rog nang.

ཁྱེད་རང་ཁ་པར་རྗེས་ལ་གཏང་རོགས་གནང་།

Do you have any message?
jag-len ga-re yo-pey.

སྐྱག་ལེན་ག་རེ་ཡོད་པས།

Call me at this number?
kha-par ang-drang dhi-thog nga-la drel-wa nang-rog.

ཁ་པར་ཨང་གྲངས་འདི་ཐོག་ང་ལ་འབྲེལ་བ་གནང་རོགས།

My telephone number is 231156.
ngey kha-par ang-drang nyi-sum-chig-chig-nga-druk rey.

ངའི་ཁ་པར་ཨང་གྲངས་གཉིས་གསུམ་གཅིག་གཅིག་ལྔ་དྲུག་རེད།

I will call back later.
nge je-la kha-par tang-go.

ངས་རྗེས་ལ་ཁ་པར་གཏང་གོ

Dialogue-VI

Where is the post office?
drag-khang ga-wa yo-rey.

སྦྲག་ཁང་ག་པར་ཡོད་རེད།

Take a two minute walk down this street.
sang-lam dhi-gyudh gom-pa kar-ma nyi gyab-na leb-gi rey.

སྲང་ལམ་འདི་བརྒྱུད་གོམ་པ་སྐར་མ་གཉིས་རྒྱབ་ན་སླེབས་ཀྱི་རེད།

I want to mail this.
nga yi-gi dhi tang-go yodh.

ང་ཡི་གེ་འདི་གཏང་དགོས་ཡོད།

Airmail?
nam-drag yin-pey.

གནམ་སྦྲག་ཡིན་པས།

127

No, sea mail.
tsso-drag yin.

མཚོ་སྦྲག་ཡིན།

How many days will it take to reach USA?
a-ri jor-ye nyi-ma ga-tssodh gor-gi rey.

ཨ་རི་སྦྱོར་ཡེ་ཉི་མ་ག་ཚོད་འགོར་གྱི་རེད།

15 days.
nyi-ma cho-nga.

ཉི་མ་བཅོ་ལྔ།

Do you want it registered?
yi-gi dhi dheb-kyel je-gi yin-pey.

ཡི་གི་འདི་དེབ་སྐྱེལ་བྱེད་ཀྱི་ཡིན་པས།

Yes. Of course.
yin-dha-yin.

ཡིན་ད་ཡིན།

How much does it weigh?
jidh-kog ga-tssodh dhug.

ཇིད་གོག་ག་ཚོད་འདུག

It weighs one kilo.
ki-lo chig dhug.

ཀི་ལོ་གཅིག་འདུག

Dialogue-VII

Where is the dry-cleaner?
log-thrus gyab-khen ga-wa yo-rey.

སློག་འཁྲུས་བརྒྱབ་མཁན་ག་པར་ཡོད་རེད།

What do you want?
khye-rang ga-re go.

ཁྱེད་རང་ག་རེ་དགོས།

I want to dry clean this shirt.
ngey todh-thung dhi tru-go yodh.

ངའི་སྟོད་ཐུང་འདི་བཀྲུ་དགོས་ཡོད།

128

Take this receipt.
ngul-zin dhi khyer-rog nang.

དངུལ་འཛིན་འདི་འཁྱེར་རོགས་གནང་།

Give us some advance money.
nga-tssor ngul tog-tsam dha-ta ngon-la tre-rog nang.

ང་ཚོར་དངུལ་ཏོག་ཙམ་ད་ལྟ་སྔོན་ལ་སྤྲད་རོགས་གནང་།

When can I get it back?
todh-thung ga-dhus tssur ra-gi rey.

སྟོད་ཐུང་ག་དུས་ཚུར་རག་གི་རེད།

Tomorrow. 6 o'clock.
sang-nyin gon-dhag chhu-tssodh druk-pa-la.

སང་ཉིན་དགོང་དག་ཆུ་ཚོད་དྲུག་པ་ལ།

You haven't washed this properly.
yag-po trus min-dhug.

ཡག་པོ་བཀྲུས་མིན་འདུག

Please wash this again.
go-nes tru-rog nang.

ཡང་བསྐྱར་བཀྲུ་རོགས་གནང་།

The buttons are broken.
theb-chi kha-shes chhag-dhug.

ཐེབ་ཅི་ཁ་ཤས་ཆག་འདུག

There is a stain here.
dhey-la nag-thig gos-shag.

དེ་ལ་ནག་ཐིག་འགོས་ཤག

I am not paying you.
ngul tre-gi min.

དངུལ་སྤྲད་ཀྱི་མིན།

Dialogue-VIII

How far is Dhondup photo studio?
dhon-drub par-khang ga-wa yo-rey.

དོན་གྲུབ་དཔར་ཁང་ག་པར་ཡོད་རེད།

129

It is just around the corner.
gyab dhi-ga rang-la.

རྒྱབ་འདི་ག་རང་ལ།

I want a roll of colour film.
nga-la phing-shog tsson-thra-chen chig tre-rog.

ང་ལ་ཕིང་ཤོག་ཚོན་ཁྲ་ཅན་གཅིག་སྤྲོད་རོགས།

Do you develop films.
khye-rang phing-shog tru-gi yo-pey.

ཁྱེད་རང་ཕིང་ཤོག་བཀྲུ་གྱི་ཡེ་ཡོད་པས།

Yes.
yodh.

ཡོད།

Does it take long?
mang-po gor-gi re-pey.

མང་པོ་འགོར་གྱི་རེད་པས།

It takes two days.
nyi-ma nyi gor-gi rey.

ཉི་མ་གཉིས་འགོར་གྱི་རེད།

Do you rent cameras?
khye-rang par-ches yar-gi yo-pey.

ཁྱེད་རང་དཔར་ཆས་གཡར་གྱི་ཡོད་པས།

No, we don't.
mey. yar-gi mey.

མེད། གཡར་གྱི་མེད།

Dialogue-IX

I want to visit Sherabling monastery in Bir.
nga Bir She-rab-ling gon-pa-la dro-go yodh.

ང་པིར་ཤེས་རབ་གླིང་དགོན་པ་ལ་འགྲོ་དགོས་ཡོད།

It is about 4 hours journey by bus.
ba-si nang chhu-tssodh shhi-rey.

སྦ་སི་ནང་ཆུ་ཚོད་བཞི་རེད།

130

I will hire a taxi.
nga mo-tra les-ye yin.

ང་མོ་ཊ་གླས་ཡེ་ཡིན།

Come with me.
khye-rang ngey nyam-dhu shog.

ཁྱེད་རང་ངའི་མཉམ་དུ་ཤོག

Why?
ga-re je-ga.

ག་རེ་བྱེད་ག

You can be my guide and translator.
khye-rang ngey ke-gyur dhang lam-ton-pa ji.

ཁྱེད་རང་ངའི་སྐད་བསྒྱུར་དང་ལམ་སྟོན་པ་བྱིས།

Are there any short cuts to Bir?
gyog-lam yo-re-pey.

མགྱོགས་ལམ་ཡོད་རེད་པས།

The road is very rough.
gyog-lam yag-po yo-ma-rey.

མགྱོགས་ལམ་ཡག་པོ་ཡོད་མ་རེད།

We will leave at dawn.
nga-tsso shhog-pa nam lang-dhus dro-go.

ང་ཚོ་ཞོགས་པ་ནམ་ལངས་དུས་འགྲུ་དགོས།

Yes. It will be cool then.
rey. dhey-dhus sil-po yo-rey.

རེད། དེ་དུས་བསིལ་པོ་ཡོད་རེད།

Dialogue-X

I am leaving on Thursday.
nga sza lhak-pa-la thon-ye yin.

ང་གཟའ་ལྷག་པ་ལ་འཐོན་ཡེ་ཡིན།

Where?
ga-wa-la.

ག་པར་ལ།

To Delhi and then back to USA.
dhang-po dhi-li. dhi-nes A-ri-la.

དང་པོ་རི་ལི། འདི་ནས་ཨ་རི་ལ།

Do you plan to come back?
khye-rang tssur pheb-tsis yo-pey.

ཁྱེད་རང་ཚུར་ཕེབས་རྩིས་ཡོད་པས།

I don't know.
dhan-ta ha go-gi min-dhug.

ད་ལྟ་ཧ་གོ་གི་མིན་འདུག

May be after three years.
chig-je-na lo-sum je-la yong-gi yin.

གཅིག་བྱས་ན་ལོ་གསུམ་རྗེས་ལ་ཡོང་གི་ཡིན།

Keep in touch.
drel-wa nang-rog.

འབྲེལ་བ་གནང་རོགས།

Where is kokonor travel agency?
ko-ko-nor drim-drul les-khang ga-wa yo-rey.

ཀོ་ཀོ་ནོར་འགྲིམ་འགྲུལ་ལས་ཁང་ག་པར་ཡོད་རེད།

It is located behind this temple.
lha-khang dhi gyab-la yo-rey.

ལྷ་ཁང་འདི་རྒྱབ་ལ།

Can you book a taxi for me tomorrow?
nga-la sang-nyin mo-tra chig go-dhug.

ང་ལ་སང་ཉིན་མོ་ཊ་གཅིག་དགོས་འདུག།

Where are you going?
khye-rang ga-wa pheb-ye yin.

ཁྱེད་རང་ག་པར་ཕེབས་ཡེ་ཡིན།

To the airport.
nam-thang-la.

གནམ་ཐང་ལ།

When?
ga-dhus.

ག་དུས།

8.30 p.m. Tomorrow.

sang-nyin gon-dhag chhu-tssodh gye-dhang chhe-ka-la.

སང་ཉིན་དགོང་དག་ཆུ་ཚོད་བརྒྱད་དང་ཕྱེད་ཀ་ལ།

Driver, please stop smoking.

tha-ma ma-thung-rog nang.

ཐ་མག་མ་འཐུང་རོགས་གནང་།

Can you please reduce the volume?

ke chung-tsam tang-rog nang.

སྐད་ཆུང་ཚམ་གཏང་རོགས་གནང་།

This is the latest Hindi pop number.

gya-gar shhe sar-shos dhi-rey.

རྒྱ་གར་གཞས་གསར་ཤོས་འདི་རེད།

I want peace.

nga-la shhi-dhe go-dhug.

ང་ལ་ཞི་བདེ་དགོས་འདུག

VOCABULARY

Ant
drog-ma   གྲོག་མ།

Bamboo
nyug-ma   སྙུག་མ།

Bat
tsi-tsi kam-po   ཙི་ཙི་སྐམ་པོ།

Bear
dhom   དོམ།

Bee
dhug-drang   དུག་སྦྲང་།

133

Bird

ja

བྱ།

Branch

yel-ga

ཡལ་ག

Buffalo

ma-ye

མ་ཧེ།

Camel

nga-mong

རྔ་མོང་།

Cat

shhi-mi

ཞི་མི།

Climate

nam-shis

གནམ་གཤིས།

Cloud

trin-pa

སྤྲིན་པ།

Cow

ba-chhug

བ་ཕྱུགས།

Crane

trung-trung

ཀྲུང་ཀྲུང་།

Cuckoo

khu-yug

ཁུ་བྱུག

Deer

sha-wa

ཤ་བ།

Dog
khyi
ཁྱི།

Donkey
bung-gu
བོང་བུ།

Earthquake
sa-yom
ས་གཡོམ།

Elephant
lang-chhen
གླང་ཆེན།

Fish
nya
ཉ།

Flood
chhu-log
ཆུ་ལོག

Flower
me-tok
མེ་ཏོག

Fly
drang-ma
སྦྲང་མ།

Forest
shing-nag
ཤིང་ནག

Fox
wah
ཝ།

Goat
ra
ར།

Grass

tsa ཙ།

Hill

ri རི།

Holly hock

ha-lo ཧ་ལོ།

Horse

ta ཏ།

Island

ling-thren གླིང་ཕྲན།

Insect

bu བུ།

Jackal

khyi-chang ཁྱི་སྤྱང་།

Juniper

shug-pa ཤུག་པ།

Landslide

sa-rus ས་རུས།

Lake

tsso མཚོ།

Leaf

lo-ma ལོ་མ།

Lotus
pe-ma པད་མ།

Marigold
gur-kum གུར་ཀུམ།

Monkey
piu སྤྲེའུ།

Moon
dha-wa ཟླ་བ།

Mountain
gang-ri གངས་རི།

Oak
ber-to བེར་དོ།

Ocean
gya-tsso རྒྱ་མཚོ།

Owl
wug-pa འུག་པ།

Ox
ḻang-kog གླང་ཀོག

Peacock
ḏa-ja རྨ་བྱ།

Pig
phag-pa ཕག་པ།

Pine
thang-shing
ཐང་ཤིང་།

Rabbit
re-bong
རི་བོང་།

Rhododendron
tag-ma
སྟག་མ།

River
tsang-po
གཙང་པོ།

Sheep
lug
ལུག

Sky
nam
གནམ།

Snake
drul
སྦྲུལ།

Star
kar-ma
སྐར་མ།

Sun
nyi-ma
ཉི་མ།

Tent
gur
གུར།

Thrush
jol-mo
མཇོལ་མོ།

138

Tree

shing ཤིང་།

Turtle

rus-bel རུས་སྦལ།

Willow

chang-ma གཅང་མ།

Wolf

chang-kyi སྤྱང་ཀི།

Village

drong-seb གྲོང་གསེབ།

13

Discovering Lhasa

The Potala

Who built Potala Palace?
po-ta-la sus shheng-pa rey.

པོ་ཏ་ལ་སུས་བཞེངས་པ་རེད།

Potala Palace was built by the Fifth Dalai Lama.
gyal-wang ku-threng nga-pey shheng-pa rey.

རྒྱལ་དབང་སྐུ་ཕྲེང་ལྔ་པའི་བཞེངས་པ་རེད།

When?
ga-dhus.

ག་དུས།

During the second half of 17th century.
dhus-rab chu-dhun gi kyil-tsam-la.

དུས་རབས་བཅུ་བདུན་གྱི་དཀྱིལ་ཚམ་ལ།

Can we visit Potala tomorrow?
sang-nyin nga-tsso po-ta-lar dro-na drig-gi re-pey.

སང་ཉིན་ང་ཚོ་པོ་ཏ་ལར་འགྲོ་ན་འགྲིག་གི་རེད་པས།

Tomorrow it is closed.
sang-nyin go-gyab yo-rey.

སང་ཉིན་སྒོ་རྒྱབ་ཀྱི་རེད།

Drepung monastery

How many monks live here?
dhey-la dra-wa ga-tssodh yo-rey.

དེ་ལ་གྲྭ་བ་ག་ཚོད་ཡོད་རེད།

140

I am a Buddhist.

nga nang-pa yin.

ང་ནང་པ་ཡིན།

What religious order is this monastery?

gon-pa dhi chhos-lug ga-re rey.

དགོན་པ་འདི་ཆོས་ལུགས་ག་རེ་རེད།

Can I go upstairs?

yar dro-na drig-gi re-pey.

ཡར་འགྲོ་ན་འགྲིག་གི་རེད་པས།

I am on pilgrimage.

nga nes-jel-la yong-wa yin.

ང་གནས་མཇལ་ལ་ཡོང་བ་ཡིན།

What is this deity called?

lha dhi ming-la ga-re rey.

ལྷ་འདི་མིང་ལ་ག་རེ་རེད།

Gyantse city

How far is Gyantse from Lhasa?

lhasa nes gyantse bar thag-ring-los ga-tssodh rey.

ལྷ་ས་ནས་རྒྱལ་རྩེ་བར་ཐག་རིང་ལོས་ག་ཚོད་རེད།

It is 395 km from Lhasa.

lhasa nes kilometre sum-gya gu-chu go-nga rey.

ཀི་ལོ་མི་ཊར་གསུམ་བརྒྱ་དགུ་བཅུ་གོ་ལྔ་རེད།

In which direction?

chhog ga-wa yo-rey.

ཕྱོགས་ག་པར་ཡོད་རེད།

It is situated west of Lhasa.

lhasa nes nub-chhog-la yo-rey.

ལྷ་ས་ནས་ནུབ་ཕྱོགས་ལ་ཡོད་རེད།

What is there to see in Gyantse?

gyang-tse-la ta-gyu ga-re yo-rey.

རྒྱལ་རྩེ་ལ་ལྟ་རྒྱུ་ག་རེ་ཡོད་རེད།

There is a fort and two very old monasteries.

zong chig dhag gon-pa nying-pa nyi yo-rey.

རྫོང་གཅིག་དང་དགོན་པ་རྙིང་པ་གཉིས་ཡོད་རེད།

A Tibetan village

What crops do you sow in the field?

shhing-ge nang-la ton-tog ga-re tab-gi yodh.

ཞིང་གའི་ནང་ལ་སྟོན་ཏོག་ག་རེ་བཏབ་ཀྱི་ཡོད།

Barley and peas.

nes dhang tre-ma.

ནས་དང་སྲན་མ།

Do you keep any dogs?

khye-rang tsso khyi nyar-gi yo-pey.

ཁྱེད་རང་ཚོ་ཁྱི་ཉར་གྱི་ཡོད་པས།

We have only one dog.

nga-tsso-la khyi chig yodh.

ང་ཚོ་ལ་ཁྱི་གཅིག་ཡོད།

When is harvest time?

tse-ma nga-wey dhus-tssodh ga-dhus rey.

བཙས་མ་བརྔ་བའི་དུས་ཚོད་ག་དུས་རེད།

It is in Autumn.

ton-ka la-rey.

སྟོན་ཀའི་ནམ་དུས་ལ་རེད།

A Tibetan nomad camp

What is this tent made of?

gur-dhi ga-re szos-pa rey.

གུར་འདི་ག་རེས་བཟོས་པ་རེད།

This tent is made of yak-hair.

gur-dhi yak-gi pus szos-pa rey.

གུར་འདི་གཡག་གི་སྤུའི་བཟོས་པ་རེད།

142

Do you have any neighbours?

khye-rang tssor khyim-tsse me-pey.

ཁྱེད་རང་ཚོར་ཁྱིམ་མཚེས་མེད་པས།

They live 100 km away.

khong-tsso kilometre gya-yi sa-char yo-rey.

ཁོང་ཚོ་ཀི་ལོ་མི་ཏར་བརྒྱས་ས་ཆར་ཡོད་རེད།

How many yak do you have?

yak ga-tssodh yodh.

གཡག་ག་ཚོད་ཡོད།

We have 10 yaks.

yak chu yodh.

གཡག་བཅུ་ཡོད།

Mount Kailash

What do you call Mount Kailash in Tibetan?

kailash-la bodh-ke nang ga-re rey.

ཀེ་ལཱ་ལ་བོད་སྐད་ནང་ག་རེ་རེད།

We call it Gang Rinpoche.

gang rin-po-che rey.

གངས་རིན་པོ་ཆེ་རེད།

Is this your first time to Mount Kailash?

khye-rang gang rin-po-cher yong-wa theng dhang-po
yin-pey.

ཁྱེད་རང་གངས་རིན་པོ་ཆེར་ཡོང་བ་ཐེངས་དང་པོ་ཡིན་པས།

This is my tenth.

theng chu-pa yin.

ཐེངས་བཅུ་པ་ཡིན།

You came by bus to Mount Kailash?

ba-si nang yong-wa yin-pey.

བ་སི་ནང་ཡོང་བ་ཡིན་པས།

I came here by doing full length prostrations.

kyang-chag tssel-nes yong-wa yin.

རྐྱང་ཕྱག་འཚལ་ནས་ཡོང་བ་ཡིན།

143

Monlam prayer festival

Who started this festival?

dhus-chen dhi sus go-tsug-pa rey.

དུས་ཆེན་འདི་སུས་འགོ་བཙུགས་པ་རེད།

This festival was started by Tsongkhapa.

je Tsong-kha-pa chhen-pos go-tsug-pa rey.

རྗེ་ཙོང་ཁ་པ་ཆེན་པོས་འགོ་བཙུགས་པ་རེད།

When?

ga-dhus.

ག་དུས།

In 1409.

chig-tong shhi-gya gu-la.

གཅིག་སྟོང་བཞི་བརྒྱ་དགུ་ལ།

So it is very old?

je-na nying-pa shhe-dra rey.

བྱས་ན་རྙིང་པ་ཞེ་དྲག་རེད།

It is about 600 years old.

lo druk-gya-yi nying-pa rey.

ལོ་དྲུག་བརྒྱའི་རྙིང་པ་རེད།

VOCABULARY-I

Directions
chhog   ཕྱོགས།

East
shar   ཤར།

West
nub   ནུབ།

North
jang   བྱང་།

144

South
lho
ལྷོ།

Northeast
jang-shar
བྱང་ཤར།

Northwest
nub-jang
ནུབ་བྱང་།

Southeast
lho-shar
ལྷོ་ཤར།

Southwest
lho-nub
ལྷོ་ནུབ།

Left
yon
གཡོན།

Right
ye
གཡས།

Centre
kyil
དཀྱིལ།

Far
thag-ring-po
ཐག་རིང་།

Near
dram-la
འགྲམ་ལ།

Top
tse
རྩེ།

145

Bottom

shodh

གཤོད།

Above

gang-la

སྟེང་ལ།

Below

wog-la

འོག་ལ།

Front

dhun

མདུན།

Back

gyab

རྒྱབ།

Corner

szur

ཟུར།

Upper

todh

སྟོད།

Middle

bar-ma

དབར་མ།

Lower

medh

སྨད།

VOCABULARY-II

Abbot

khen-po

མཁན་པོ།

Bonpo
bon-po
བོན་པོ།

Butter lamp
chhod-me
མཆོད་མེ།

Carpet
drum-se
གྲུམ་རྩེ།

Geluk
ge-luk
དགེ་ལུགས།

Incarnate lama
trul-ku
སྤྲུལ་སྐུ།

Monastery
gon-pa
དགོན་པ།

Monk
dra-wa
གྲྭ་བ།

Nunnery
a-ni gon-pa
ཨ་ནེ་དགོན་པ།

Nyingma
nying-ma
རྙིང་མ།

Offering
chhod-bul
མཆོད་འབུལ།

Sakya
sa-kya
ས་སྐྱ།

Sect
chhos-lug ཆོས་ལུགས།

Statue
ku-dra སྐུ་འདྲ།

Temple
lha-khang ལྷ་ཁང་།

Thangka
thang-ka ཐང་ཀ

Monasteries in Tibet

Ganden
ga-dhen དགའ་ལྡན།

Drepung
dre-pung འབྲས་སྤུངས།

Sera
se-ra སེ་ར།

Tashilhunpo
ta-shi lhun-po བཀྲ་ཤིས་ལྷུན་པོ།

Kumbum Jampaling
ku-bum jam-pa-ling སྐུ་འབུམ་བྱམས་པ་གླིང་།

Labrang Tashikhyil
lab-rang ta-shi-khyil བླ་བྲང་བཀྲ་ཤིས་འཁྱིལ།

Sakya
sa-kya ས་སྐྱ།

Tsurpu
tssur-pu

ཚུར་ཕུ།

Mindroling
min-dro-ling

སྨིན་གྲོལ་གླིང་།

Yungdrungling
yung-drung-ling

གཡུང་དྲུང་གླིང་།

Tibetan cities

Lhasa
lha-sa

ལྷ་ས།

Shigatse
shhi-ga-tse

ཞིས་ཀ་རྩེ།

Gyantse
gyang tsc

རྒྱལ་རྩེ།

Chamdo
chham-dho

ཆབ་མདོ།

Dartsedo
dhar-tse-dho

དར་རྩེ་མདོ།

Golmud
ker-mo

གེར་མོ།

Rebkong
re-kong

རེབ་གོང་།

Chabcha
chhab-chha

ཆབ་ཆ།

Gyalthang
gyal-thang   རྒྱལ་ཐང་།

Nagchu
nag-chhu   ནག་ཆུ།

Rivers in Tibet

Drichu
dri-chhu   འབྲི་ཆུ།

Machu
ma-chhu   རྨ་ཆུ།

Zachu
za-chu   རྫ་ཆུ།

Ngomchu
ngul-chhu   རྒྱལ་མོ་རྔུལ་ཆུ།

Senge Khabab
sen-ge kha-bab   སེང་གེ་ཁ་འབབ།

Tachog Khabab
ta-chhog kha-bab   རྟ་མཆོག་ཁ་འབབ།

Maja Khabab
ma-ja kha-bab   རྨ་བྱ་ཁ་འབབ།

Langchen Khabab
ang-chhen kha-bab   གླང་ཆེན་ཁ་འབབ།

Lakes in Tibet

Kokonor
tsso ngon-po

མཚོ་སྔོན་པོ།

Tso Mapham
tsso ma-pham

མཚོ་མ་ཕམ།

Yamdrok Yutso
yam-drok yu-tsso

ཡར་འབྲོག་གཡུ་མཚོ།

Namtso
nam-tsso

གནམ་མཚོ།

Kyaring Tso
kya-reng tsso

སྐྱ་རིང་མཚོ།

Ngoring Tso
ngo-reng tsso

སྔོ་རིང་མཚོ།

Lhamo Lhatso
lha-mo lha-tsso

ལྷ་མོའི་བླ་མཚོ།

Mountains in Tibet

Kailash
gang rin-po-chhe

གངས་རིན་པོ་ཆེ།

Everest
jo-mo lang-ma

ཇོ་མོ་གླང་མ།

Nyenchen Thangla
nyen-chen thang-la

གཉན་ཆེན་ཐང་ལྷ།

Amnye Machen
am-nye ma-chhen

ཨ་མྱེས་རྨ་ཆེན།

Machen Pomra
ma-chhen pom-ra རྨ་ཆེན་སྤོམ་ར།

Yarlha Shampo
yar-lha sham-po ཡར་ལྷ་ཤམ་པོ།

Minyag Gangkar
mi-nyag gang-kar མི་ཉག་གངས་དཀར།

Rongtsen Khawa Karpo
rong-tsen kha-wa kar-po རོང་བཙན་ཁ་བ་དཀར་པོ།

Gangkar Chokley Namgyal
chog-ley nam-gyel མཆོག་ལས་རྣམ་རྒྱལ།

Gangkar Shamed
gang-kar sha-mey གངས་དཀར་ཤ་མེད།

Jomo Khareg
jo-mo kha-reg ཇོ་མོ་མཁའ་རེག

Tibetan animals

Yak
yak གཡག།

Dri (female yak)
dri འབྲི།

Dzo (cross between a yak and cow)
zo མཛོ།

Drong (wild yak)
drong འབྲོང་།

Kiang (wild ass)
kyang རྐྱང་།

Druk (mythical serpent-like creature)
druk འབྲུག

Senge (mythical snow-lion)
seng-ge སེང་གེ།

Tibetan diet

Tsampa (roasted barley flour)
tsam-pa རྩམ་པ།

Thukpa (soup)
thuk-pa ཐུག་པ།

Momo (stuffed meat dumplings)
mo-mo མོག་མོག།

Pag (tsampa moistened with tea and kneaded into balls)
pag སྤགས།

Boja (Tibetan butter tea with salt)
bodh-ja བོད་ཇ།

Tingmo (dumplings)
ting-mo ཏིང་མོ།

Chura (dried cheese)
chhu-ra ཆུར།

Chang (barley beer)
chhang ཆང་།

14

What, where, when, who and how?

What?
ga-re   ག་རེ།

Where?
ga-wa   ག་པར།

When?
ga-dhus   ག་དུས།

Which?
ga-dhi   ག་འདི།

Who?
su   སུ།

How?
ga-dre-si   ག་འབྲས་སི།

What is your name?
khye-rang ming ga-re yin.
ཁྱེད་རང་མིང་ག་རེ་ཡིན།
What is this?
dhi ga-re rey.
འདི་ག་རེ་རེད།
What did you say?
khye-rang gi ga-re lab yin-pey.
ཁྱེད་རང་གི་ག་རེ་ལབ་ཡིན་པས།

154

What shall I do now?
dha-nga ga-re ji-ga.

དང་ག་རེ་བྱེད་ག

What is the matter?
ga-re je-song

ག་རེ་བྱུས་སོང་།

What do you want?
khye-rang la ga-re go.

ཁྱེད་རང་ལ་ག་རེ་དགོས།

What is your mother's name?
khye-rang a-mey ming-la ga-re rey.

ཁྱེད་རང་ཨ་མའི་མིང་ག་རེ་རེད།

What is your profession?
khye-rang chhag-les ga-re nang-gi yodh.

ཁྱེད་རང་ཕྱག་ལས་ག་རེ་གནང་གི་ཡོད།

What do you mean?
khye-rang ga-re lab-gi yodh.

ཁྱེད་རང་ག་རེ་ལབ་ཀྱི་ཡོད།

What is the name of this place?
sa-cha dhi-ming ga-re rey.

ས་ཆ་འདིའི་མིང་ག་རེ་རེད།

What did you say?
ga-re sung yin-pey.

ག་རེ་གསུང་ཡིན་པས།

What do you charge?
gong ga-tssodh len-gi yodh.

གོང་ག་ཚོད་ལེན་ཀྱི་ཡོད།

What time does the office open?
les-khung ga-dhus go chhe-gi rey.

ལས་ཁུངས་ག་དུས་སྒོ་ཕྱེ་ཡི་རེད།

What is tsampa?
tsam-pa szer-na ga-re rey.

རྩམ་པ་ཟེར་ན་ག་རེ་རེད།

What is your telephone number?
khye-rang gi kha-par ang-drang ga-re rey.

ཁྱེད་རང་གི་ཁ་པར་ཨང་གྲངས་ག་རེ་རེད།

What is the charge per day?
nyi-ma chig-gi la-cha ga-tssodh rey.

ཉི་མ་གཅིག་གི་གླ་ཆ་ག་ཚོད་རེད།

What is my room number?
ngey khang-mig-gi ang-drang ga-tssodh rey.

ངའི་ཁང་མིག་གི་ཨང་གྲངས་ག་ཚོད་རེད།

What special food do you serve?
kha-lag mig-sel ga-re szo-gi yodh.

ཁ་ལག་དམིགས་གསལ་ག་རེ་བཟོ་ལི་ཡོད།

What time do you close?
ga-dhus go gyab-gi yodh.

ག་དུས་སྒོ་རྒྱབ་ཀྱི་ཡོད།

What is the name of that mountain?
ri pha-gi ming ga-re rey.

རི་ཕ་གི་མིང་ག་རེ་རེད།

What is the name of this monastery/
gon-pa dhi ming ga-re rey.

དགོན་པ་འདིའི་མིང་ག་རེ་རེད།

What is the price of this/
cha-la dhi gong ga-tssodh rey.

ཅ་ལག་འདིའི་གོང་ག་ཚོད་རེད།

What do you want to buy?
khye-rang ga-re nyo-ge.

ཁྱེད་རང་ག་རེ་ཉོ་གས།

What is the best time to visit this place?
sa-cha dhir yong-ye dhus-tssodh yag-shos ga-dhus rey.

ས་ཆ་འདིར་ཡོང་ཡི་དུས་ཚོད་ཡག་ཤོས་ག་དུས་རེད།

What is the time?
chhu-tssodh ga-tssodh rey.

ཆུ་ཚོད་ག་ཚོད་རེད།

What time are you going?
khye-rang chhu-tssodh ga-tssodh-la dro-ge.

ཁྱེད་རང་ཆུ་ཚོད་ག་ཚོད་ལ་འགྲོ་གས།

What time will you return?
khye-rang chhu-tssodh ga-tssodh-la log-ge.

ཁྱེད་རང་ཆུ་ཚོད་ག་ཚོད་ལ་ལོག་གས།

What is the date today?
dhey-ring tsse-drang ga-re rey.

དེ་རིང་ཚེས་གྲངས་ག་རེ་རེད།

Where are you going?
ga-wa dro-ge.

ག་པར་འགྲོ་གས།

Where do you stay?
ga-wa shhug-gi yodh.

ག་པར་བཞུགས་ཀྱི་ཡོད།

Where can I buy newspaper?
tssag-par nyo-sa ga-wa rey.

ཚགས་པར་ཉོ་ས་ག་པར་རེད།

Where is the post office?
drag-khang ga-wa rey.

སྦྲག་ཁང་ག་པར་རེད།

Where is the library.
pe-zodh ga-wa rey.

དཔེ་མཛོད་ཁང་ག་པར་རེད།

Where can I find you?
khye-rang ga-wa nye-gi rey.

ཁྱེད་རང་ག་པར་རྙེད་ཀྱི་རེད།

Where is shop no.5?
tssong-khang ang nga-pa ga-wa rey.

ཚོང་ཁང་ཨང་ལྔ་པ་ག་པར་རེད།

Where is the bus stand?
bas ti-sing ga-wa rey.

རྣངས་འཁོར་འབབ་ཚུགས་ག་པར་རེད།

157

Where is the taxi stand?
mo-tra bab-tssug ga-wa rey.

མོ་ཊ་འབབ་ཚུགས་ག་པར་རེད།

Where is Dhondup restaurant?
dhon-drub sza-khang ga-wa yo-rey.

དོན་གྲུབ་ཟ་ཁང་ག་པར་ཡོད་རེད།

Where is Passang Hotel?
pa-sang dron-khang ga-wa yo-rey.

པ་སངས་མགྲོན་ཁང་ག་པར་ཡོད་རེད།

Where is Ngodup video parlour?
ngo-drup video ta-sa ga-wa rey.

དངོས་གྲུབ་སློག་བརྙན་ཁང་ག་པར་ཡོད་རེད།

Where can I get chang?
chhang ga-wa ra-gi rey.

ཆང་ག་པར་རག་གི་རེད།

Where is the hospital?
<u>m</u>en-khang ga-wa rey.

སྨན་ཁང་ག་པར་རེད།

Where shall we stop?
nga-tsso ga-wa ka-ge.

ང་ཚོ་ག་པར་བཀག་གས།

Where can I find her?
mo ga-wa <u>ny</u>e-gi rey.

མོ་ག་པར་རྙེད་ཀྱི་རེད།

Where can I buy medicines?
<u>m</u>en nyo-sa ga-wa rey.

སྨན་ཉོ་ས་ག་པར་རེད།

Where did you go?
khye-rang ga-wa chhin-pey.

ཁྱེད་རང་ག་པར་ཕྱིན་པས།

Where were you yesterday?
khye-rang dhang-gong ga-wa chhin-pey.

ཁྱེད་རང་མདང་གོང་ག་པར་ཕྱིན་པས།

158

Where is your friend?
khye-rang gi drok-po ga-wa.

ཁྱེད་རང་གི་གྲོགས་པོ་ག་པར་ཡོད།

Where is my bag?
ngey cha-lag ga-wa chhin-song.

ངའི་ཅ་ལག་ག་པར་ཕྱིན་སོང་།

When did you come?
ga-dhus ļeb-pey.

ག་དུས་སླེབས་པས།

When are you leaving?
ga-dhus dro-ye yin.

ག་དུས་འགྲོ་ཡི་ཡིན།

When does the bus leave for Lhasa?
ba-si dhi ga-dhus Lha-sar dro-gi rey.

རྐྱང་འཁོར་འདི་ག་དུས་ལྷ་སར་འགྲོ་ཡི་རེད།

When did you open?
ga-dhus go chhe-pey.

ག་དུས་སྒོ་ཕྱེ་པས།

When do you close?
ga-dhus go gyab-gi yodh.

ག་དུས་སྒོ་རྒྱབ་ཀྱི་ཡོད།

When can I get my passport back?
ngey pa-si ga-dhus tssur ra-gi rey.

ངའི་པ་སི་ག་དུས་ཚུར་རག་གི་རེད།

When should I come?
nga ga-dhus yong-ga.

ང་ག་དུས་ཡོང་ག

When are you coming?
khye-rang ga-dhus yong-ge.

ཁྱེད་རང་ག་དུས་ཡོང་གས།

When shall we leave?
nga-tsso ga-dhus thon-ge.

ང་ཚོ་ག་དུས་ཐོན་གས།

When shall we stop?
nga-tsso ga-dhus tssam shhag-ge.

ང་ཚོ་ག་དུས་མཚམས་བཞག་གས།

When should I start?
ga-dhus go tsug-ga.

ག་དུས་འགོ་བཙུགས་ག།

When will they come?
kho-tsso ga-dhus yong-gi rey.

ཁོང་ཚོ་ག་དུས་ཡོང་གི་རེད།

When did she go?
mo-rang ga-dhus chhin-song.

མོ་རང་ག་དུས་ཕྱིན་སོང་།

When will we reach Lhasa?
nga-tsso ga-dhus lha-sar jor-gi rey.

ང་ཚོ་ག་དུས་ལྷ་སར་སྦྱོར་གྱི་རེད།

When does the party start?
tro-kyi ga-dhus go tsug-gi rey.

སྤྲོ་སྐྱིད་ག་དུས་འགོ་བཙུགས་ཀྱི་རེད།

Which is my room?
ngey khang-mig ga-wa rey.

ངའི་ཁང་མིག་ག་པར་རེད།

Who are you?
khye-rang su yin-pey.

ཁྱེད་རང་སུ་ཡིན་པས།

Who is that girl?
bu-mo pha-gi su-rey.

བུ་མོ་ཕ་གི་སུ་རེད།

Who is that person?
mi pha-gi su-rey.

མི་ཕ་གི་སུ་རེད།

Who is with you?
khye-rang nyam-dhu su-yodh.

ཁྱེད་རང་མཉམ་དུ་སུ་ཡོད།

160

How are you?
khye-rang ga-dre dhug.

ཁྱེད་རང་ག་འདྲས་འདུག

How many people were there?
mi ga-tssodh dhug.

མི་ག་ཚོད་འདུག

How will you go?
khye-rang ga-dre-si dro-ge.

ཁྱེད་རང་ག་འདྲས་སི་འགྲོ་གས།

More Language Books
from
Pilgrims Publishing

- A Concise Dictionary-Newar-English .... S Iswarnand
- A Course in Nepali .... David Matthews
- Bhasha bhi: Sahitya Bhi .... K C Bhatia and P S B Shilansu
- Dictionnaire Francais- Nepali ..... Evelyn Chazot and Soma Pant
- Dizionario Italiano Nepalese .... A Lovatti and P Gondoni
- Grammar of Colloquial Tibetan .... Sir Charles Bell
- Hindi phrase Book: A Pilgrims Key to Hindi .... Paul Wagner
- Nepali Phrase book: A Pilgrims key to Nepali. .... R Josephson
- Tibet Phrase Book: A Pilgrims key to Tibetan .... Kerry Moran
- Tibetan-English Dictionary .... Sarat Chandra Das

www.pilgrimsbooks.com

For Catalog and more Information, Mail or Fax to:

PILGRIMS BOOK HOUSE

Mail Order, P.O.Box 3872, Kathmandu, Nepal
Tel: 977-1-424942 Fax: 977-1-424943
E-mail: mailorder@pilgrims.wlink.com.np